Praise for
TAPESTRY

There is such a depth of soul found in these pages that the reader feels a profound obligation to simply be present to them, suspending judgment and evaluation as their luminosity shimmers and resonates in the reader's own soul. This is a book to be cherished and returned to again and again.

—**MICHAEL MARTIN**, poet, philosopher, and author of *The Submerged Reality: Sophiology and the Turn to a Poetic Metaphysics*

I marvel at the broad and deep knowledge displayed by this wise man. His openness and compassion shine through the text. Ultimately this is a book about spirituality, deeply rooted in Christian faith but open to the insights of other traditions. I'm grateful to Bishop Seraphim for his generosity in sharing the treasures he has gathered over a lifetime of ministry and reflection.

—**FR. JOHN L. BOSTWICK, O. PRAEM.**, Canon of St. Norbert Abbey, Spiritual Director

Here Merlin meets Einstein, E. E. Cummings meets Enoch, and there is a decided bias towards apophatic theology. God is seen through Nothingness, or through the Black Paintings of Ad Reinhardt, which the author calls holy cathedrals. No fundamentalism here. No rigid theology. For the adventurous only, the curious, for those who search. For the unorthodox Orthodox.

—**PETER VON BERG**, Actor/Director/Acting Teacher

While staying rooted in his Orthodox faith and his personal encounters, Bishop Seraphim ponders offerings from an astonishing array of writers, teasing out the ways they match or overlap or contradict each other. His ultimate pursuit, it seems, is nothing less than how we find and know and understand the higher purposes of God.

—**MICHAEL N. MCGREGOR**, author of
Pure Act: The Uncommon Life of Robert Lax
and International Thomas Merton Society board member

Tapestry by the highly esteemed Eastern Orthodox Bishop Seraphim Sigrist, is exactly that—a collection of explorations involving the philosophy of religion, several light touches of Jungian Psychology, and various literary and biographical diversions, of which "Fr. Alexander Men and Saint Nikolai" is particularly moving and inspiring. Read through, there is an Ariadne's thread that pulls it all together into a coherent whole. A brilliant piece of work and a must for the serious student interested in fathoming a deeper realization of life in our distracted, literalistic, and troubled times.

—**JOHN N. H. PERKINS** has practiced for many years
as a psychoanalyst in the tradition of C. G. Jung.
He is the author of *Rapture Alive:*
Living the Legend of the Holy Grail, and
Soul Loss: Life Lessons from the Tragic Tale of Undine.

TAPESTRY

Bishop Seraphim Sigrist

LUMIN ⊙ PRESS

ISBN: 978-0-9987710-4

Published by Lumin Press
Clinton, New Jersey
Printed in the United States of America

CONTENTS

PREFACE

"A POET IS FIRST OF ALL, someone who sees the world in a different way, someone who has his own secret theme." Father Alexander Schmemann, who wrote this, was a theologian, but a theologian who recorded in his journals that there was more theology in a volume of the poet E. E. Cummings, than in a pile of theology books on his desk beside it. He himself certainly had his own themes, a poetic center around which his writings circle.

After I wrote the book titled *The Theology of Wonder*, I found, in the process of moving to a new home, some writings of mine transcribed by my mother and dated by age. It seems that when I was four I spoke a poem, which began:

> "The world is turning
> Roundabout, roundabout,

Turning toward the stars.
This is the magic song of the stars—
The song of the wonder of the world..."

I had forgotten this writing but I remember also at some very young age thinking that I saw things in a way which, if I could but put it into words, would extend the understanding people had. It seemed that what I wanted to express concerned the relations of objects in the visual field.

Many years later I would find Proust speaking of the mystery for which he could not find words when, as a child, he noted the relations in space of three church spires altering as the carriage he was riding in moved and turned. The sense "that something more lay behind that mobility, that luminosity, something which they seemed at once to contain and to conceal."

Growing a little older I gained vocabulary and learned to write without a crayon, and then with a typewriter, but I found as all people do, that becoming an adult and having more words did not really bring all the new understanding I might have expected. If anything, the intuitions, the themes, came to seem more as if a half-heard music than like something I could put in words.

Yet perhaps I have had, and have yet, some themes
. . . and so it is to work with them, and to express them,
and by work and expression perhaps again to find
them, that I have written this little book.

A composer whose work I love, Anton Webern, late in
life would scrawl symbols on a napkin or paper in a
cafe and say that it was not important to transcribe
them into notes because they were meta-music—a
music which he heard and which, in time, everyone
would hear.

I cannot say that I hear this music, really, certainly not
at all clearly. But I hope these writings, gathered into
this Tapestry, will serve as sign of a music I could never
transcribe or play, and yet, sensing its presence, perhaps
I may share that sense with the reader.

I

THE SHEEP'S SHOP

THE SHEEP'S SHOP is in Oxford at 33 St. Aldate's, but before arriving there, we have a few stops on the way.

1. TWO YEARS AGO AT A CONFERENCE in Scotland, I enquired about a friend, who also was my godson, whom I had known in Japan, and I was told he had rather recently, it seems, committed suicide. Yesterday, however, I met someone who had known him more continually over the years and was told that he had died in the night apparently of a heart attack and at a moment of hope and some achievement in a life which indeed, his friend told me, might have been earlier ended by himself. He was a sensitive young man with a very wild and fantastical sense of humor, gifted in arts but, as I remember him, not easily fit for this world, maybe. So I was happy to hear, as it

seems, that in his life he had come to a new place, learned indeed a new language and was with a friend in a new land. But life is full of mysteries as to, if not what happened, then what might have happened, isn't it?

I recall this friend, then young decades ago, had liked David Bowie in *Labyrinth* ... perhaps in some way corresponding to the forking paths of lives ... and perhaps it is not only to Bowie seeking love but in the end even more to the infant who is saved from the labyrinth to whom his destiny corresponded.

2. C.S. LEWIS AT THE END of his dream fiction *The Great Divorce* has his narrator see in a reverie:

"... a great assembly of gigantic forms all motionless, all in deepest silence, standing forever around a little silver table and looking upon it and on the table were little silver figures like chessmen who went to and fro doing this and that. And I knew that each chessman was the 'idolum' or puppet representative of some one of the great presences that stood by. And the acts and motions of each chessman were a moving portrait, a mimicry or pantomime, which delineated the inmost nature of its gigantic master. And these chessmen are men and women as they appear to themselves and to one another in the world. And the silver table is Time. And those who stand and watch are the immortal souls of those same men and women."

Does this satisfy as a view of what human persons are? That is to say, what is that greatness which makes the person a gigantic figure when seen beside that person in Time? Lewis' thought seems unclarified perhaps? As stated, I find the vision interesting and suggestive but needing development.

3. THE VITRUVIAN MAN OF LEONARDO shows man as proportional to the universe, extended against the 360 degrees of the circle. It may indeed be that somehow if "like is known to like," that the universe of our perception is proportional to our measure.

4. MARCEL PROUST AT THE END of his monumental novel *In Search of Lost Time* sees each person as a figure of immense stature, a giant in the flow of Time. Like the old church at Combray built and added to over so many periods, each person in his or her serial selves becomes an immense figure in Time, something far more than what we see in each other and ourselves in our daily perspective.

5. THE SHEEP'S SHOP was the candy store in Oxford which John Tenniel immortalized in his illustrations of Lewis Carroll's *Through the Looking Glass*. Alice Liddel came to this shop as a little girl in the 1850s to buy sweets. Here Alice finds herself faced with a bewildering array of objects that shift and vanish as she looks at them. Finally, she buys an egg from the shop's owner who is a sheep. But in picking up the egg she finds she must follow it through the depths of the store which become a woods which become a new place entirely in which the egg is Humpty Dumpty by whose wall she is standing. We suggest that if she had chosen another object to purchase, a different story would have followed.

6. CERTAIN IT IS that in our lives we at each moment make large and small choices leaving path after path unchosen which would have been possible. Nicholas de Cusa suggests that all that is possible is real in the mind and plan of God but only some of this possible is actualized in history.

7. THIS IS DISTINCT from the Many Worlds Interpretation of quantum physics, which proposes branching re-

alities. I suppose it could be more like Leibniz's rather unfortunately expressed suggestion (setting himself up for Voltaire and Candide) that there are countless possible worlds of which God actualizes only "the best of all possible worlds." For Nicholas the possibilities related to each individual, things that one might have done and been and, on the other hand, things that might have happened to one and around one in life, are stated as real in the mind of God but not as pertaining to the persons themselves.

However, just as we may see a person as having an immense extension in the series of selves in Time, we may also see each person as being the center of an immeasurable number of possibilities, which in some way relate to that person.

> What we desire travels with us
> We must breathe time as fishes
> Breathe the water
> God's flight circles us.
> —Denise Levertov

8. THIS CAN HAVE AN ASPECT as one thinks of it of recovery of what was not realized within Time:

Thy gentle dreams, thy frailest,
Even those that were
born and lost in a heartbeat,
Shall meet thee there.
They are become immortal
in shining air.
>   —A.E. (George W Russell)

9. HOWEVER, NOT ALL UNREALIZED POSSIBILITIES are of course simply our loss. Anyone who drives a car knows how close one comes to accidents or if a little heavy footed or careless, how often one gets away without a possible ticket and so on. This leaves our line of thought, were at left at that, subject to the sort of demolition Plato has Parmenides, in his most mysterious dialogue the *Parmenides*, effect on all simple expressions of his own doctrine of Forms.

10. THE IMMEASURABLE POSSIBILITY of which you or I are center and which in some way pertains to us, perhaps can only be synthesized into one within life as we live it. Perhaps this is the meaning of T.S. Eliot's words, "What might have been and what has been point to one end which is always present."

11. FURTHER, CONCEIVED EVEN IN THIS WAY, it may be objected that the person, however, in one aspect immeasurable and almost infinite in extent, nonetheless, rests on nothingness and the abyss of nonbeing from which it rose.

In one aspect this is the place where a life, already in Time and in the immeasurable range of its possibilities touching infinity, accepts its negation in order to realize itself again, still individual yet so within the whole of Life itself, which for a Christian is understood as participation in the Resurrection.

12. BUT RETURNING TO THE SHEEP'S SHOP, now we find ourselves in a world of mysterious choices; choice required by the dimension of Time at the point where the possibilities and actuality meet.

However, perhaps with a realization of an immensity still greater maybe than that of Lewis's giant figures, but not, as they seem in relation to the chessmen on the silver board of Time, external to us, rather as the depth beyond comprehension of that being given us drawn from and inseparable from Being itself.

II

MICHAEL

NOVEMBER 8 IN THE EAST OF CHRISTIANITY is the day of St Michael and all the angels, corresponding to Michaelmas in the West on September 30.

Angel means messenger. A messenger brings a communication from one to another and the more accurately he transmits it the better of course. So in old days the role of representative, for example when Abraham wished to find a bride for Isaac from people in his old country of Sumer, he sent a personal representative or *shaliach*. "A man's *shaliach* is even as himself," is the old saying, and so the representative with Abraham's full trust and authority finds Rebekah to come back with him. The word *shaliach* underlies the Greek apostle, and so when Paul says that the Galatians received him as if he were the Lord he is speaking from this idea . . . and the bishops of the church in some measure bear this same role of, at times, speaking with apostolic authority. However, what is true even with a human *shaliach*, that the message will be a little changed, is the more true with our communication in general that sooner or later our messages passed on lose their authenticity and become that distortion that the game of telephone illustrates. So the importance of the angel in our faith begins with this: that the message is fully transmitted from God, and the angel, adding nothing personal, embodies the message . . . indeed we know nothing at all personal about the angels (which does not mean they may not be persons but simply that for us they are the message).

Some messages are for many people to receive and for all to know, and these are embodied in the archangels such as Michael, Gabriel and Raphael in the Bible and perhaps the others, Uriel and still others whose names are added elsewhere. . . . We again know nothing personal about Michael the Archangel but we know him as, well in the early east in Constantinople he was the message of healing, but elsewhere and as time went on he is progressively associated with divine authority against evil. "Holy Archangel Michael defend us in this battle . . ." and churches of St Michael in many places are atop mountains which may primitively have been regarded as gates to the underworld, and so he stands guard. Gabriel we know as pure essence of message to Mary, to Zachary to Daniel . . . a sign of mercy and Incarnation; Raphael as healer of Tobit. Uriel is not Biblical but John Milton says that he in the Sun is the eye of God. Then there is Metatron, Prince of the countenance, but we get beyond what we can handle today or perhaps ever.

God is so personal that even, it seems, his messages are personal . . . does this mean that we ourselves are, as each a message from God into the world, angels? Not perhaps exactly, but this does lead to the second sort of angelical being which is what we call the guardian angel. It is the belief of Christians with some Biblical base as, "Do not despise one of these little ones, for I say to you that their angels in heaven continually see the face of My Father," and in our prayer for "an angel of peace," that each soul corresponds to a "guardian angel." Though there is no definition in dogma, it is our faith that God sends a message to each person which is our angel. Surely that angel is first of all the realization of the self God created us to become and be. Our individual "contract" which, as novelist Saul Bellow says, each of us deep down knows. A contract not as written, but, as Jeremiah foretells, a covenant of the heart present in personal form. For this reason, the angel is our guide and guardian because he is that into which we are becoming, and guardian and assurance of our link, through that irrevocable call of God, to eternal life.

The angel shepherd and keeper of our being... "Where kept? Do tell us where kept, where? Yonder —what high as that! We follow now we follow. Yonder—yes yonder, yonder, Yonder."

Perhaps we may say also that the Guardian Angel, as shepherd of being, is the one (if anyone is and if the line of thought be appropriate) in whom all the possibilities, what might have been and what has been, all the forking paths which make up our life-way are gathered up and resolved.

And the tower of St Michael on the tor, the hill, at Glastonbury, said to be the gate of the underworld, itself stands without roof open to the sky, rooted in the depth of time, the angelical open to a future God discloses and which is not now limited within time. In this unlike the parish church at Combray, which for Marcel Proust represented a journey through the countless moments of history and Time but with no perceived opening, except memory and imagination, beyond Time.

So the day of Michael is that of all named for that Archangel but in including all the angels, I suppose, really, also it becomes the day of all of us. We whose angels stand always before God and also on the way as our guides and as our most intimate relation to the Lord. Realizing this we may enter also a new awareness of ourselves as those through whom God reaches out into the world . . . as we act to defend, show mercy, heal and help others, we ourselves are living that angelic life to which we are called.

Or in the words of psychologist John N Perkins, "With this realization of the angelic depth of life, we find a reenchantment of all experience," and in the words of the hymn by John Henry Newman may say, "With the morn those angel faces smile/ which I have loved long and lost a while."

III

THE DELICACY OF ENDINGS

FRANK HERBERT'S SCIENCE FICTION EPIC *Dune* begins with the thought that "beginnings are very delicate times." No doubt that is so but endings too have their delicacy don't they? Indeed, taking the example of *Dune*, the author continued the original novel through 5 sequels, and his successors after his death have added prequels and sequels so that it is a sort of franchise without definable beginning or end either.

Clement of Alexandria (c150–c215) started his last collection of writings called *Stromata*, Miscellanies or *Patchwork* or *Tapestry* it could be translated, with the intention of completing an orderly presentation of his thought, though with modulation—the sort of modulation a gentle, erudite but somewhat all over the place theologian with an attraction to the esoteric might propose. "Some things my treatise will hint; on some it will linger; some it will merely mention. It will try to speak imperceptibly, to exhibit secretly, and to demonstrate silently." However first of all it will be systematic, he says, and then at the beginning of the fourth section he finds he has to admit that the developing work is indeed a patchwork, and far from systematic it is "patched together"—passing constantly from one thing to another, and in the series of discussions hinting at one thing and demonstrating another. "For those who seek for gold," says Heraclitus, "dig much earth and find little gold. But those who are of the truly golden race, in mining for what is allied to them, will find the much in little." Further he grants that some sections are more interesting than others but that too he gives the purpose of throwing off the not serious reader. So the work goes on through three more books or perhaps four because scholars are uncertain where his writing ends and whether the compilation of the eighth book is by Clement at all.

Books whose end point is on the face of it obvious also have their delicacies of ending. The book of Job ends with the voice of God speaking from a whirlwind and giving the book's final thought on the mystery of suffering. But reading those last chapters, 38-42, make the experiment of then reading chapter 28. Although chapter 28 can be thought of as a continuation of words given Job in the previous chapter, scholars feel that it is likely an independent composition of the overall author but written separately and then included in the book at this point.

Where is wisdom he asks? it seems one can delve the depths of the earth and pass through the dark night of the inner earth and ask even death and death does not know. We are reminded of the Rig Veda 10:129 on the origin of creation. "But, after all, who knows, and who can say Whence it all came, and how creation happened? . . . Whence all creation had its origin, he, whether he fashioned it or whether he did not, he, who surveys it all from highest heaven, he knows—or maybe even he does not know."

Job 28 says that wisdom is indeed in God but in its fullness beyond the knowledge of death or of life and this seems to me as an ending more majestic and full than the final chapters and in a sense the best ending of the book, an ending which might incidentally have forestalled Carl Jung's *Answer to Job*, but . . . But this is not to say that it is a disarrangement of chapters rather that there can be an appropriate arrangement with a somewhat hidden but other conclusion.

Marcel Proust's great novel cycle *Remembrance of Things Past* (or in search of lost Time) ends with the sense of the immensity of individual persons in the dimension of Time But it is a little earlier when he, or rather the viewpoint character, is sitting in a library waiting to be called to a concert hall opposite and experiences, at the striking of a spoon against cup reminding of a sound heard in a train and the opening into depth beyond calculation, the obliteration of Time and of Death which is the goal of the novel, and then called to the concert and leaving the library he returns to Time and the everyday where death has still the dominion.

The placing is appropriate or necessary in the structure of the work but it is there in the library that the journey ends as Samuel Beckett pointed out in his fine monograph on Proust. So the ends of things are not always at some seeming linear end of a progression but can be at any time where the deep sense of the progression becomes evident. May we say at any thin place where the light beyond visible light shines through.

IV

METATRON

ENOCH, THE SEVENTH PATRIARCH in the line from Adam, is portrayed in his brief appearance in Genesis (Gen 5:18–21) as one who had a direct and continuous relation with God, "who walked with God", and who is the first of men to not die in the ordinary sense of things but it is said, "He was not for God took him." The author of Hebrews uses him among the examples of faith (Heb. 11:5–6) saying that he pleased God and so did not die. We are told that he lived 365 years (perhaps a solar year of years indicating completion) and had sons and daughters and that is the story of Enoch. It is from the time when history was indeed story, but brief as it is, it is perhaps one of the important stories underlying the whole Biblical history on the one hand and the whole of human history on the other

C.S. Lewis observes that good though the *Odes of Pindar* are, if one were to try the experiment of daily reading from them and also from the *Psalms*, of about the same period of composition, it is certainly Pindar whom one would tire of first. Perhaps something similar holds when we think about the ancient beginnings of the idea of Theosis, of humanity becoming divine.

We might think first of the Greek heroes become divine; of Hercules or Orion, or perhaps in another cultural context of how in Japanese Shinto everything from ancestors to sacred places is '*kami*' (a god) These are indeed valuable moments within the history of religion, but the very human nature of the divinity assumed by the heroes and the animistic sense of the Shinto world view, reminds one that this is indeed within precisely "religion history."

But then there is the story of Enoch of the Old Testament in itself and also in his later development in legend and traditions into the angelical figure of Metatron which we may feel stands out as a timeless and universal contemplation of Theosis.

The presence of this story, which is seed for the later development, shows, we would suggest, that "Theosis" is not a Patristic and late Christian development, or even, though for Christians its final groundedness in Christ is certain, a New Testament concept exclusively, but it is an inward aspect of the Biblical story.

So, let us follow this development from the seed of the story. Metatron is the name given to Enoch of Genesis 5, "the seventh patriarch," as he is joined to and becomes a great angelical being—Metatron. The 3rd book of Enoch tells us, "This Enoch, whose flesh was turned to flame, his veins to fire, his eye-lashes to flashes of lightning, his eye-balls to flaming torches, and whom God placed on a throne next to the throne of glory, received after this heavenly transformation the name Metatron." The story is told in apocryphal and pseudepigraphical books 2nd and 3rd Enoch, Jubilees, and developed in Hekalothic and Kabbalistic literature until it attains a remarkable complexity. The stories of legendary figures often originate in various places and times and then merge into a single story and so it is here. So the question for us coming from the point of view of Biblical studies within the general awareness of history is why should we be concerned with Enoch-Metatron?

In reply I should like to start by setting to one side pretty much the whole lot of questions relating to sources and original purposes and to clear away many of the legendary aspects, interesting and labyrinthine as they are, and also and in particular the later Kabbalistic materials in which Metatron becomes hardly Enoch at all but a projection of an emanation of the *Shekinah* and of *Malkuth*, the cosmos as mirror of all the lights above, in the Kabbalistic flow chart of creation and tell the story that remains, which is perhaps the heart of it all, and its reason for being and for remaining among human stories. And, indeed, it is a story which I would say is a natural meditation and development of the Scriptural verses on Enoch.

Let us tell the story as:

Before history began there was a man called Enoch. We are told he "walked with God", lived a full life and had sons and daughters. One son was Methuselah who gets into a George Bernard Shaw play.

Enoch did not study science as we know it, did not know theology or literature, had not read Shakespeare or Niels Bohr, had not sat under Gotama's tree or seen Dante's rose, but somehow, as the story tells us, he understood and could express the deep laws of creation in the fullness of his person which he grew into, perhaps growing beyond the time he walked in his dawn world but still having the identity and personhood of Enoch to which was added a new name.

Leaving aside the complicated details of the development of the idea of Metatron from the Enoch of Genesis, we are left with his titles and his roles as a human grown into the angelical world. Of these, we will refer in passing to others but focus on two or three which seem to me central, the role of measurement and of recording of the acts of God and the title of "*Na'ar* (The Youth)."

The name he was called by of Metatron is linked to measurement. He was in a sense the measurement of the world so perfectly was he fitted to it.

And perhaps he was the *Shiur Komah*, the measurement of God as present in the worlds of the universe. Metatron's extent measures the extent of the *Kabod*, of the Glory which fills all things, we are told, in one place.

"I was enlarged and increased in size until I matched the world in length and breadth" (III Enoch) and in another place "The stature of this youth fills the world."

This is what is said of him, but it is no more than what Leonardo or Shakespeare thought of humanity, or what Barrow and Tipler teach as the Anthropic Principle in Cosmology. In brief that the "universal physical constants" lead to human life.

The world is the right home for humanity. We fit it, and our measurement measures and fits its form. We are capable at our full extent, and beyond logics and learning, or like Enoch prior to them, of knowing from within the laws of the worlds and of meeting, as like meets like, the maker of the worlds because we share that which he pours into Being: Life. Life of God equal to Life of humanity.

This is what we might call the "Sign of Metatron," and of Leonardo's image of "Man according to Vitruvius," (that famous drawing of the human form extended against a circle and square). In the East it fits to the thought of Church Fathers like St Maximus for whom man was (Lars Thunberg's expression)"Microcosmos and Mediator." It is the sign of the world's fit, and measured in human life. It is always dawn in the world of true measure because one can only measure what exists, and at every moment the only realities are beginnings as the Eternal makes the worlds ever anew and sustains them in Time.

So Enoch is sign of the dawn; youth, measurement, the fullness of humanity at home in the worlds.

And most of all he is that Mystery of humanity as at home in Time and redeeming Time.

"What is your name?" Metatron answers, "I have seventy names, corresponding to the seventy tongues of the worlds ... but my King calls me 'Youth' (Na'ar)."

Analytic psychology speaks of the dual archetype, "*senex et puer,*" age and youth, this can become part of our image of God . . .

"The One is also younger than itself" in the shimmering words of Plato.

This two-sided image indeed begins in God, but as archetype it is also our sense of what it is to be human or what it should be and can be to be human. For we have the longing to join experience to innocence, what was to what is and to what shall be, but a hard wisdom will say in the words of C. R. Ramuz:

> You have no right to share
> What you are with what you were.
> No one can have it all,
> That is forbidden.

This is a bitter wisdom, but is it the final word of wisdom?

Time in its movement, its being the arrow of time, its apparent irreversibility, seems to be a losing, an evanescence, and we experience it as such and yet we also experience every moment as newness as a uniqueness just beginning. This is our experience of Time.

The word square, Sator Arepo Tenet Opera Rotas (one possible reading of the meaning of which might be "the maker, God, sustains his works in all the spheres.") which reads the same forward and back, up or down was loved by Anton Von Webern—we would say precisely because it is the magical equilibrium of Time at repose and disclosed and this is what is the aspiration of Webern's music, and indeed the Sator square moves in time forward and back in his Opus 24 as he wrote to his friend Hildegard Jone.

Enoch-Metatron lives a year of years, three hundred and sixty-five, in the iconic words of the story from the dawn of our world, and so it is he who is the Elder and yet as Metatron he is also the Youth. In his person, in the story, he is the springing free of Time played out in Webern's "music of the future."

Now we may say that for a Christian the fulfillment of the antinomy of youth and age and beginning and end is of course within God and within Christ who in the Apocalypse says, "I am Alpha and Omega. The first and the last." And who as a babe in Bethlehem was both the maker of the worlds at each moment and yet receiving them and experiencing them for the first time.

But this fulfillment and resolution of the Mystery of Time is not in Christ as something alien to humanity, but rather, and this is what the story of Metatron shows, it is as the image of the fullness of humanity and as the full dimension and natural possibility of our life, ultimately and even here and now in the depth of our humanity, that depth touched by Enoch who lived a year of three hundred and sixty five years and who is the youth and the recorder, for as we said only the youngest can record that which is ever new—the creation of the world in Time.

In Metatron we see the image of the answer to Nicodemus, on how he can be born again before all preconceptions, hopes and fears; and his story illustrates the Buddhist central concept of "*Shoshin*, "Beginner's Mind," the mind that knows without mediation.

So if the titles and offices of Metatron which are many (as he said 70, one for each of the worlds), can be analyzed in terms of the history of the development of "Metatron" yet taken as a whole they are the deep dimension of the work of humanity, as we have said of the humanity envisioned by Leonardo or by contemporary scientists as the Anthropic Principle in Cosmology . . . They range like a radius drawn from the center of all things to their edge and back, which is to say they are the multiple levels of human being. Metatron is the recorder and the memory. He is the discloser of the secrets of the worlds He is intercessor uttering the voice of the created to the creator and of the creator to the worlds.

In him we see the presence and the face of the Eternal He is therefore the Liturgy of all things and the priest He is time in its ever newness all moments in their beginning. He is the Measure of all and in his full stature measures the Image of Eternity. Metatron is, in short, what else than you and I and all of us in our full humanity. He is the inner truth of what it is to be human. Metatron is Theosis. Becoming-As-Divine.

So this is what the story of Metatron comes to, to an image of life in its fullness. But as we look up from the story we may feel with a touch of sadness that it is not the story we are living. We have our experience of life and of time but not often of its resurrection. We have come a long way but are not at the place of beginnings. Or are we? Granted that the best of stories may leave us with a task, yet in this case, perhaps the task is at least partly to, "know what we know," what is implicit in our own deep personhood, and to enter, by that knowledge, the story of Enoch/Metatron.

In any case a story which can make such a proposal is surely one worthy of being told and heard, and so we have tried to hear it and tell it.

V

A VISIT WITH RYOKAN

"THIS MORNING I woke up very early
And I saw the dark
Running along behind the trees.
Then I saw a little door
Open in a cloud

And the sun walked in."

I composed this poem, likely among my best writing until now, at age four and my mother transcribed it.

A while back I showed the poem to old Ryokan, or Ryokan Taigu, Ryokan the Fool as he called himself, the 19th-century poet and hermit and he smiled and offered me a cup of sake and said: "why don't your write another one now from further down the road?"

"Is there a road? I have heard it said that there is no obstacle and there is no way."

Ryokan laughed and slapped his knee "I've heard that too! but by gum there is a way and you know it!"

As I nod, Ryokan leans forward and says softly and as it were confidingly: "Just open a door in the first cloud on the right tomorrow morning and start from there!"

"And where does the way go?"

"Why that's easy! right back where you always walk . . . and maybe to my door with a poem?"

He struck a comic pleading tone.

And one of these days I will do it.

VI

BLAISE

THESE NOTES, revised and added to a little, began a few
years ago when I saw a survey asking the reader what
character in an original non-English book one would
choose to be, my just about first thought was Blaise in
Robert de Boron's *Story of Merlin*. It is written in Old
French even though the characters are somehow British
and of course also allowing it to be fundamentally fictional. Well, this got me to thinking a bit about Blaise,
who sort of came to mind out of the blue (or maybe out
of some inner cloudiness of course) and here I propose
to gather what material I have and find about this figure,
about the Blaise of the story of Merlin, who does indeed
interest me and I think perhaps may interest you as well.

Blaise was, Robert de Boron (c 1200A.D.) tells us, the
confessor of Merlin's mother from before the birth of

Merlin whose father it seems was an aerial spirit.(Laya-
mon's account)—in appearance a handsome young
man but of the sort that Apuleius tells us live between
the earth and the moon and indeed she never saw him
again.

The circumstances of the birth on the one hand lead
to a severe questioning of his mother whom Blaise pro-
tects, and on the other hand mark the son as a walker
between the worlds. Blaise, from the first, recognizes
the remarkable character of the son, and it is he who is
asked by Merlin to undertake to write a book which
will be a story of the Grail and also of Merlin's own
words, and it is Merlin's intention that this book be
joined to a book of Joseph of Arimathea provided by
Merlin, and Merlin says, "When the two books are put
together there will be one beautiful book, and the two
books will be one and the same."

We are told that Merlin chose Blaise because he was a
"good clerk and subtle," and says "because I am dark
and always be, let the book also be dark and mysterious
in the places where I will not show myself."

He tells Blaise that he will have to endure much for the
undertaking, though Merlin more, and that while Merlin walks the world furthering his plan (which involves

the Kingdoms of the world and the Grail and the unit-
ing somehow of this world to that which is Coming
and so ending the terrible times of history—to put it
perhaps a little beyond the immediate concept of the
author but perhaps not, it does seem to be what Merlin
is saying) Blaise will go to the north to the place of the
Wardens of the Grail, and he will have the burden of
his writing not being known, but the consolation of
being with the Wardens and also in the end, although
in an indirect way, among the "companions of the Grail
as you should be," and, thereafter and beyond that, *joie
peredurable,* "eternal joy."

In the so called *Didot Perceval* there is this: "Blaise said,
'Merlin, you told me that when these works were completed you would put me in the company of the Grail.'
and Merlin answered him, 'Blaise know that you will
be there by tomorrow.'"

Beyond that there is little in de Boron or in what is
called the "post vulgate" cycle account about Blaise except the repeated pattern of Merlin visiting Blaise who
is described sometimes as "his (Merlin's) master" or his
mentor I suppose, and recounting everything for Blaise
to write down. A typical expression is, "Merlin took
leave of them and went straight to Blaise, and told him
all those things, and Blaise put them all down and that

is how we know them." But I do not suppose that it can be understood that Robert de Boron's book or any of the others is intended to *BE* the Book of Blaise, still less the One Book made from the combining of his book with the one held by Merlin which is "one and the same" yet the two together the One Book . . .

It is in the deep northern forests that Merlin visits Blaise. We may see Merlin as harking back to the time of the druids when all was oral rather than written allowing his work to enter the new time through the writing down by Blaise.

The role of Blaise can be seen in various ways, as a scribe, a sort of Boswell, whose life is given to recording a great adventure in which he participates by that recording. Or, on another hand, occultists sometimes, it seems, see him as a mage himself and a coworker or even guide to Merlin in his plan. In one, he is "the inner self of Merlin." My reading of it would be that Blaise's role is more modest, that the birth of Merlin, for example, was not the result of his plan (as that of Arthur will be of Merlin's) but that likely he is conceived (since after all it is more story than history) an advisor of Merlin with whom Merlin thought together . . . Rather as Gandalf—who surely owes much to Merlin in his character—will visit and talk with some in

Rivendell or in Lorien or among the Ents or with Tom Bombadil.

In any case, Blaise's role is modest but it is not that of a pure observer and he also has his quest even if it is not that of a Knight, the quest as it may be of a sort of Mage or of, more essentially, a sort of Priest...

Of the end of Blaise, we hear nothing but as A E Waite says in his overwritten, as all his work, but fine account of these things, "We infer that Blaise was taken into the choirs of heaven according to the promise of Merlin and is, therefore, in *la Joie Perdurable*...

It is possible that the figure of Blaise is a combination of elements, and this is part of what gives it such complexity as it has—Blaise as the priest Merlin's mother went to, Blaise as a somewhat shadowy figure behind Merlin, Blaise as scribe—I see suggestions that as scribe he is originally the historical Welsh writer Bleheris, the only 12th century bard whose name remains to us and who seems to have known many elements of the Grail stories. But of course any interesting character can be made from various elements by an author, so Father Zosima of *The Brothers Karamazov* is based in part on particular historical people, and partly is invention.

In that branch of the story which brings Merlin to his relationship with Vivian (Nimue) who uses his own magic to confine him outside of our space, Blaise rebukes Merlin on his way to his new love. "But when Merlyn tho spake of his paramour thanne abasched hym sore Blayse..." (Huth Merlin). I prefer the branch of the story of the Didot Perceval where Merlin retires to his *esplumoir*, (that uniquely used mysterious old French word literally something like "molting place") and Blaise to his place among the Company of the Grail.

And Blaise came to Perceval, the story tells now of a meeting other than with Merlin, and indeed to the place of the Grail, for it says Perceval had the Grail in his keeping and was of "such a holy life that the Holy Ghost often descended upon him." Blaise tells Perceval, just as he had heard from Merlin, of the end of the round table and the passing of Arthur from the circles of the world.

And Merlin departs to his place with a prayer that the book of Blaise may be read and, "That our Lord would give his grace to all who willingly hear and you may say Amen."

What in Blaise do I resonate to? I suppose to that of the quest followed on a way involving intellect, and also sympathy, within the story of Blaise we are given, that of Blaise for Merlin's mother and for Merlin. He stands at one remove from the quest, as must all who live within our history and are readers of the stories, and yet is counted of its company.

As Merlin says to Blaise (De Boron) "And you, Blaise, will go to bring an end to the work you have undertaken . . . And the story will be forever told and gladly heard as long as the world lasts."

ADDITIONAL NOTES

1. How Modesty Blaise, the one might say female James Bond of comics and then novels by Peter O'Donnell, was named:

> Peter O'Donnell says in an interview, "At that time, I was reading a book by C.S. Lewis. It was called *That Hideous Strength,* and it featured the resuscitation of Merlin from the days of the Arthurian legend. It was here that I learnt that Merlin's tutor was a magician called Blaise. This was a monosyllable (as required for cadence) and it also had a fiery ring to it. So she became Modesty Blaise."

Elsewhere O'Donnell makes a back-history of Modesty's life. She started as a street waif in North Africa who grew up tough, who chooses the name after hearing the stories of Arthur and Merlin.

2. From *That Hideous Strength*, C.S.Lewis. Merlin speaking: "I had heard of it in my own days- that some had spoken with the gods. Blaise, my Master, knew a few words of that speech."

John Matthews, I expect with more literal intention, says that Blaise is apparently of "an older and more powerful order (than Merlin)," though this is not made clear in the text."

3. From *Merlin* by E.A. Robinson "[Blaise] was nigh the learnedest of hermits; His home was far away from everywhere, and he was all alone there when he died."

4. From *The Cry of Merlin the Wise*. 1498 Burgos, translated from Spanish by Dorothea Salo:

And Merlin said to Blaise, "I will be sent for from the West, and those who will come to find me swore to their lord to kill me and bring him my blood, but when they see and hear me they will not want to kill me. And when I go with them, you will go to those who have the Holy Grail, and write in this book what happened to me and what will happen from here on, and also all the deeds of the great men of this land; and this book will be in the memories of men forever and they will hear it willingly in many places."

5. From the *Prose Merlin* 15th-century English translation of Old French 13th-century of Robert de Boron:

Than seide Blase, "I se well that thow wilt now leve me. What wilt thow that I shalle do of this werke that I have begonne?" "That shalle I telle thee," quod Merlin . . . thow ne shalt not come with me, but by thy self, and axe after a londe that is cleped Northumbirlonde. And that contré is full of grete forestis and full wylde to them of the selve contré. Ther thow shalt abide, and I shall come to thee and telle thee all the mater that longeth to thi werke. And moche is thy travayle, and thow shalt have gode leyser; and as longe as the worlde dureth shall thi boke gladly

ben herde. And wite thow well that my grete
traveill shall not be byfore this kynges courte.
This kynge, to whom all my grete traveill shall
be, and the traveile of Grete Breteyne, his name
shal be Arthur. Thow shalt go thider, as I have
told thee, and I shall often come to thee and
brynge soche tidinges as thow shalt put in thi
boke. And wite it well,peple shul be glad ever
to heiren it. For shul but fewe thinges be don
but in no place, but therin shal e a partye. And
thi boke shal be cleped while the worlde en-
dureth the Boke of the Seynt Graal."

6. From an interview with Jane Yolen, "This is the kind
of thing (bringing together characters who lived half a
millennium apart) that you did in the first story of
Merlin's *Booke*, where Geoffrey of Monmouth and
Blaise meet..."

7. Susan Wilson Youkins, in *Heirs of Fate*, has Blaise
under an apple tree tutoring Arthur, Gawain and others
as boys, and emphasizing the importance of scientific
thought, "imagination is to be held in high respect
...but knowledge is the wing."

8. Norma Lorre Goodrich identifies Blaise with Saint Cadog, a role to which he might seem to have only a vague relation rather like that to the role of Merlin of St Dubricius whom she proposes as "the" Merlin.

9. John Matthews writes, "Behind the figure of Merlin, shadowy and insubstantial as a ghost stands that of his 'master' Blaise, portrayed sometimes as a monk or hermit, but always as older and deeper sunk in the wells of time. Few have succeeded in making contact with him. Those who do are possessed of a potential access to the entire Grail corpus . . . See him as a monkish figure in a brown habit, seated in a whitewashed cell poring over a beautifully illuminated tome. What does that book have to tell?"

FINALLY

And you, Blaise, will go to bring an end to the work you have undertaken; you won't come with me, but you will go off by yourself and ask the way to a land called Northumberland. The land is full of great forests, and it is forbidding even to those who belong there, for there are places where no one has yet been. And you will live there. And I'll come to you and tell you all the things you need to make the book you have begun. You must work hard at it, for you will have great rewards from it: during your life you will have a full heart, and at the end, everlasting joy. And the story will be forever told and gladly heard as long as the world lasts.

Blaise as we know him is a figure of literature, perhaps a composite of more than one story, but now as John Matthews says we see him as if having an unexpected reality and life. Of course any character if focused on acquires a certain life, and some have a uniqueness which makes them somehow like archetypes, more real in some respect than the people we meet daily. Don Quixote, Sherlock Holmes, Mister Micawber... Figures involved in the Grail Quest such as Galahad and Perceval and Merlin have this sort of immortality. The case of Blaise is a little different. He is as much observer as participant in the Quest. He observes and records because it is his own only possible way to the Grail. In so doing he stands in relation to the Grail Quest where we do, at a remove and hearing it as a story—he from Merlin and we, as it were, from him. In this way he breaks the "fourth wall" of the theater doesn't he, as surely as do Pirandello's *Six Characters in Search of an Author*, and stands with us having bypassed Robert de Boron or any other intermediate, if fully historical from the beginning, author. Perhaps this is the achievement of his quest as much as his coming to the place of the Grail, and it is achieved by his desire to incarnate into the story, to become one of the Companions...He passes into *la Joie Perdurable* not simply as someone written in a book, but as himself writer and of our company as well as of the Company of the Grail.

VII

DETECTIVE AND PRIEST

FR. MICHAEL MEERSON writes of visiting Fr. Men and finding him engaged in watering the lawn with a hose in one hand and holding in the other a book—Dante's *Commedia* in Italian. Fr. Men explained to Fr. Michael that he had almost memorized it and needed it every day. The image is attractive, of caring for the garden and engaging the mind at once, it seems a sort of expression of divine wisdom doesn't it? And we can understand the importance of Dante for a priest or for any Christian. Now it is another aspect of Fr. Alexander's reading which I should like to speak of briefly. the utility of which may be not quite so immediately apparent, and that is his pleasure in detective stories, and perhaps we could also include his interest in science fiction, but that would be to cast our net a little too broadly, although I might mention here that I am told he preferred hard science fiction such as that of Isaac Asimov, to fantasy. But limiting ourselves to detective stories and without much concrete information except that he enjoyed Father Brown and Agatha Christie and so on, I think perhaps we can offer one or two suggestions as to how these interests dovetail with his work as priest.

First though let us allow that for anyone the reading of detective stories offers a relaxation, and we must allow any priest, even as devoted a one as Fr. Alexander, what we grant ourselves, the motive and the possibility of reading for pleasure. Although if we ask just what is relaxing and enjoyable about detective fiction we may come around in the end to something serious.

1.

NOW WE MIGHT START by asking what is the detective, of detective fiction? It might seem that the question is self-evident in its answer, that he is simply a portrait with imagined narrative of actual detectives. But fiction is not usually realistic in that sense is it? For all the persuasive detail of the 19th century whaling industry in *Moby Dick* it is not likely that there were many captains of whalers resembling Captain Ahab. And Raymond

Chandler known for very realistic, "hard-boiled," detective fiction says in a letter:

> "The private detective of fiction is a fantastic creation who acts and speaks like a real man. He can be completely realistic in every sense but one, that one sense being that in life as we know it such a man would not be a private detective..."

What would he have been? It is interesting to speculate about Chandler's Philip Marlowe with his pint of whisky always at hand, his solitary replaying of the chess games of Jose Capablanca, his reading of T.S. Eliot, his tenderness, idealism, toughness and loneliness... of course he might have been an author of detective fiction but otherwise it is not clear... But perhaps we find an important clue in the case of George Simenon's Inspector Maigret, who by the way was a favorite of Fr. Alexander Schmemann.

In *Maigret's First Case,* we are told about the basis of Maigret's career in the police that, "Even as a young man, in his village, he had always had the impression that a great many people were not in their rightful place, that they were following a path which was not their own, simply because they didn't know better." It seems that Maigret chose to enter the police because it was closest to the profession he had always desired, "a profession that really didn't exist." He imagined a man, "very intelligent and full of understanding both doctor and priest . . . who would understand at his first glance the destiny of the other person." People would come to consult such a person as they consult a doctor. He would be in some way a "mender of destinies." (Concerning his phrase, "Mender of Destines," Simenon remarks that as a boy he felt the profession of, for example, physician, was incomplete because he did not heal destinies—we give this in full in the third of our notes and asides following). This person would be a mender of destinies, "because he was capable of living the life of all men, of putting himself in the skin of all men." Peter Ely in *Detective and Priest: The Paradoxes of Simenon's Maigret,* points up this important passage and adds that in his identification with the poor and with the victim, Maigret, finding in the detective's work that profession which did not exist, that new path, found the role of the priest, but one, in Peter Ely's words, "Closer to the priestly role of Christ than to the clerics who would have dominated the Church of Simenon's years in Liege. If Maigret is priestly, it is according to the model of the compassionate founder of Christianity." In short whether with full intention or not, Simenon has used his detective to open out a broader vision of the role of the priest. That on the one hand, but on the other perhaps pointing to the oddity not only of the profession of the fictional detective (who as Chandler says in real life would not be a detective at all) but also to the oddity of the profession of priest as perhaps being perpetually reinvented and disclosed by priests. Fr. Alexander Schmemann said that priesthood is not a vocation like doctor or scientist or teacher or lawyer or engineer, but it is a vocation of the man with in a sense no vocation, the question mark, the pointing to something else over against all the vocations.

We can certainly say that, as a priest, Fr. Alexander Men was quite unique in his work and expression of priesthood, finding and creating a way of life and work in a way parallel to that of Simeonon's Maigret, living "a profession that really didn't exist," and this may be one deep way in which the vocation of priest and of fictional detective come together.

2.

THERE IS A MORE SIMPLE PARALLEL and practical point of meeting perhaps in their approach to people. Maigret describes the intelligence of the detective as needing to be one who understands others, "Because he is capable of living the life of all men, of putting himself in the skin of all men." Chesterton's Father Brown in *The Hammer of God* reveals to the murderer not only how his crime came about but his thought processes leading to it. The murderer, himself a vicar, asks how he knows all this, "Are you a devil?" "No I am a man, and because I am a man I have all the devils in my own heart." In *The Secret of Flambeau,* he explains that, "When I tried to imagine the state of mind in which a crime might be done I realized that I might have done it myself under certain mental conditions, and not under others . . . and then I realized who had done it." His knowledge is not, like Sherlock Holmes', of obscure poisons, etc. (though he does learn from "his little flock" in confession some odd things that come in handy) but of the human heart, starting from knowing the root of action, of good and evil in himself. This is the sort of thing that priests such as Fr. Makari of Optino said about how they have insight in hearing confessions and dealing with people, not through clairvoyance but through inner knowledge. Fr. Men would say this is how when he prepared the examen of conscience for general confession, by knowing his own heart, and so people would feel nonetheless that he was speaking directly to them. And outside confession, and in everyday relations he had that quality of being with people so attentively that each would, as Fr. Michael Meerson and many others remember, feel the almost unique friend of the priest.

3.

NOW MOVING ON AND SELECTING one more point of contact between the role of priest and that of fictional detective, we have the awareness of, and moral engagement in, the conflict of good and evil. He is what, of course, all Christians are (and so again the oddity of priesthood considered as a "vocation") in the world, and for the world; loved by God but not of that other Johannine world, the one of darkness. Raymond Chandler expresses this in his famous formulation: "Down these mean streets a man must go who is not himself mean, who is neither tarnished nor afraid. The detective must be a complete man and a common man and yet an unusual man. He must be, to use a rather weathered phrase, a man of honor. He talks as the man of his age talks, that is, with rude wit, a lively sense of the grotesque, a disgust for sham, and a contempt for pettiness." If this fits Philip Marlow, Chandler's great invention, does it not also fit a priest serving in the world of light and shadow and of Fr. Alexander Men in his work in the difficult time and society in which he lived? Well of course F. Men would not be as easily acted by Humphrey Bogart as Marlowe was, but, nonetheless, this quality of being in the world, caring for it, speaking its language and yet being neither tarnished by its stains nor afraid of its terrors, surely fits him and makes one more point of meeting of fictional detective and of priest.

4.

JUST QUICKLY AND TO BRING IN those authors whom in the field of detective fiction I myself particularly liked, the rather fantastical Michael Innes (pen name of J.I.M. Stewart) and Edmund Crispin (Bruce Montgomery) . . . they play the plots and characters over the top (perhaps rather as the TV avengers did the espionage conventions) and Jared Lobdell calls them the "farceurs." Fr. Men did not care for the fantastic in science fiction, preferring Asimov and Clarke, and I expect the same would have held with mysteries. But in these stories of Innes and Crispin I recall that clergy who appear tend to be quite surprisingly like Oxford dons, with as many tags from the classics, or thoughts on St Thomas's ontological proof, or lines from Wordsworth as Innis's Inspector Appleby has and this in spite of being but village vicars. Well of course the same paradox of surprising, to others, intelligence in a priest, is one of the aspects of Chesterton's Father Brown always surprising people who expect him to be superstitious and obscurantist etc., and Fr. Alexander Men was certainly one who surprised the expectations of many of a "village priest." Yet here again we see the role of priest as realized in life, as not being containable within expectations... like the fictional detective the priest has a vocation which is hardly a vocation at all by the standards of other vocations, as Fr Schmemann said, and yet as Maigret found is one which can bring healing and resolution to all.

5.

SO, AS TO RESOLUTION, from parallels of the role of fictional detective and actual priest we might turn finally to a quality which may go to what a priest reading these stories finds relaxing, which is also one of the things that any Christian reading detective fiction may find rewarding... and that is that really they are morality plays. Chesterton puts it in his inimitable style in the *Illustrated London News*. later reappearing in *All Things Considered*, "The inconsistencies of human nature are indeed terrible and heart-shaking things, to be named with the same note of crisis as the hour of death and the Day of Judgment. They are not all fine shades, but some of them very fearful shadows, made by the primal contrast of darkness and light. Both the crimes and the confessions can be as catastrophic as lightning. Indeed, The Ideal Detective Story might do some good if it brought men back to understand that the world is not all curves, but that there are some things that are as jagged as the lightning-flash or as straight as the sword." As Jared Lobdell, the noted Tolkien scholar, observes, detective stories are as much morality plays as were the medieval mystery plays and as such they have what Tolkien calls the quality of "eucatastrophe," precisely of good-catastrophe. This is the denouement of the detective, and it echoes what we feel is the inner truth of the world, that Christ's Incarnation is the eucatastrophe of history and the Resurrection the eucatastrophe of the Incarnation. The Christian, and the priest, finds then in detective stories such as Fr. Men loved, a relaxation which is not escapism but rather an experience of the inner truth of our world.

NOTES AND ASIDES:

1. We have only spoken of certain authors here. The works of Agatha Christie certainly have a basic moral structure, and this the more so when Poirot is played

by David Souchet and we see him praying the rosary in *Murder on the Orient Express*. Beyond that, perhaps her deepest moral and spiritual explorations are in the stories of Harley Quin, gathered in *The Mysterious Mister Quin*. These entrancing stories are an allegory of love inspired by the *commedia del arte,* and they were Christie's own favorite of all her works. Dorothy Sayer's Peter Wimsey in a way abundantly and completely fits the role of detective- priest of course but perhaps we may question whether more and more the Sayer's novels do not break out of the category of detective fiction entirely and from *Gaudy Night* into *Busman's Holiday* really become mainstream romantic novels.

2. The role of psychologist could be a third in effect triangulating that profession which does not yet exist sought by Maigret.

3. Simenon, in his *Confessions* writes, "When I was 14, I had this thought: why is there not a kind of physician who would be at the same time physician of the body and physician of the intelligence, in other words a type of physician who would know an individual, his age, his physique, his possibilities, able to advise him to follow this or that path. I was almost formulating psychosomatic medicine. This was in 1917 and it is in that spirit that I created the character of Maigret. That is

how he operates, and that is why it was necessary for Maigret to have two or three years of medicine, to give him at least a share of the spirit of medicine. Maigret is for me a mender of destinies. He is the equivalent of the men who go through the streets to mend chairs or crockery. That is what I had in mind when I was 14. I considered that the profession of physician as it was then was not complete, and that the physician was not doing all he should do. He also should be a mender of destinies."

4. John Dickson Carr's Gideon Fell is modeled in appearance on Chesterton and in some points of methodology on Father Brown, but his works seem to me in the pure puzzle genre quite different from those of Chesterton, where the plot is rather secondary.

5. The Rector in Edmund Crispin's *Glimpses of the Moon* might offer a clue as to why Crispin is called a *farceur*. "'I'm not,' the Rector had once complacently remarked, 'the type of thing you want to meet unexpectedly on a dark night.'" It is he who chooses to appear at his church fete as Madame Sosostris, Famous Clairvoyant (the character in T.S. Eliot's *Wasteland*) . . .

VIII

THE CHEMIST'S SHOP

IN THE MR. TOMPKINS BOOKS, the physicist George Gamow introduces the worlds of the atom and of quantum physics through a series of dreams by his Mr. Tompkins after attending lectures on these subjects. Perhaps somewhat in that spirit a dream or fantasia, in which perhaps after some obscure lecture on the Divine Wisdom, Sophia, one dreamed, remembering the lecturer saying that this topic is set aside by many Orthodox theologians who might grant it legitimacy if at all as a "theologumena," a more or less acceptable theological opinion, but not a central or necessary doctrine. Dreaming, one meets something like the Raymond Chandler character Philip Marlowe, played by Humphrey Bogart, in a scene of the Charles Williams metaphysical fantasy *War in Heaven*.

THE CHEMIST'S SHOP

Even a man neither tarnished nor afraid must go down the mean streets, though most people you see there look both worn and frightened, especially on a gray day, when the smog is over the city like a pall. I've been on the mean streets before but these were about the meanest I had seen. dingy, dark as the night of the soul, tasteless as a roadside blonde, a neighborhood that belonged in LA like a pearl onion does on a banana split. And I had gone down those streets for a dame before, but never for a dame like this.

She was the real thing. All I remember, and I try to remember, and trying to remember means for me taking a hit on my flask of Jack green label the kind you only get in the south, and all I remember is a vision of blue and a voice like a dulcimer and eyes you could lose yourself in they had no bottom, and the voice saying "I need some Theologumena."

I didn't know the word, but I have my DDR (Detectives Desk Reference) and I looked in it and nodded ... I began to understand...

Theologumena... that use of thought beyond the

tracks of Dogma which yet joins the dogmas in some new pattern which cannot itself be dogmatized...

If she was who I thought she was then, "I think I know why," I said.

"I heard you were a wise man, Marlow. Yes, I cannot exist without it... Will you get it for me?"

"Anything for you, Sophia" I said... It comes back ... but especially the blue... the eyes... where did they begin and where end? Heck with it. Do the job. Just another dame. And just another neighborhood, although about the worst I've seen. Couple of guys on the corner look like George Raft and the fellow in Key Largo whose name I forget... But no Lauren Bacall in sight. Glad I've got the 45 strapped under my jacket, I park the old Chevy and go into a dingy dark shop. Says "Chemist's Shop" on the window... a window which has been broken and fixed with glass that was already dirty.

"Dimitrios!" I call. The man behind the counter blends in the shadows. He looks somehow Mediterranean but some people older than the Greeks... older than the Jews...

I see it all: the candles, the incense. the bottles, the flasks, the cans, the amulets and talismeta, the swords and cups, the books . . . Balthasar . . . Barth . . . Kung . . . Rahner . . . Schmemann, John Lowell, Bernard Lonergan . . . It is dark but I see, because I have trained myself to see, some things hard to find, but not what the lady needed. All theology, all the externals of the theologic work, all the elixirs and encyclopedias but something, some whole category, missing . . . but I knew it was there. I could feel it in the air . . . still . . . electric . . .

"They say you have some out of the way things, Dimitrios," I say . . . "Nothing is out of the way," he whispers . . . t ired, watchful, a voice old and alien as Atlantis.

"The ordinary way, the way everyone goes."

"Everyone goes nowhere."

"But I go . . . You have something for me."

"What I have is for buyers."

"I have paid the price," I say, thinking of long nights replaying chess with the games of Jose Capablanca, in a tiny apartment off La Cienega.

"I have some rare things, some precious things," he whispers, "but only for for buyers."

"You know I have paid." The bourbon, the ashtrays full of Lucky Strike butts, the long lonely nights . . . Dimitrios nods and takes a large tube from under the counter. "It is the ointment."

"Theologu . . ."

"Sssh . . . the ointment . . . It is rich and scarce and strange. You have paid, but is it for you only?"

"No it is for another," I find myself saying.

"You are right to speak as you understand truly, it is for another, and she will live by this, but it is also for you for you will live by her life."

Thank . . ."

"No. Go."

I went. He vanished in the shadows. On the corner I saw a tough looking Chinaman who reminded me of an actor whose name I forget . . . Suey? Fat?

No matter. The sun was burning through the smog for the first time in the month and there was a touch of azure.

I could tell it was going to be a good day.

IX

TWO VISITS

1. NEW YORK: IRIDESCENCE

Much of the art in the house of a friend is by the children of the family and I am particularly struck by a watercolor of a village in winter. There are trees and buildings and snow and a bubble floating in the air and through which part of the scene is seen as a separate floating bubble world. It seems that the bubble world is not different from this one and yet it adds a coloration. We could imagine that the church in the bubble is not present in the external world but that seems unlikely to be intended. The tree compounded of external and bubble parts seems to fit together precisely. Yet within the bubble there is a special iridescence absent in the external village.

I suppose in some of our bubbles, that is to say of the worlds as we see them from each our unique perspectives, there may be things only hinted at in the external world, sometimes which we have developed in a wild and idiosyncratic way, sometimes which we have seen the essence of and expressed...

In table conversation among other things the book *Oblomov* by Goncharov came up. I picked it up later in Princeton at a book store and looked in it for the first time in a long time. Oblomov is a particular type, so much so that one can speak of "an Oblomov," for the most part lying on his sofa and wishing things would somehow fall into place of their own accord. His efforts to take charge of his life are fitful. The tone is gentle, sympathetic, and sad. Maybe the sadness is from the awareness of how much of life of at least many people is like this, a flow from one day to the next and one year to the next. After those made long ago...what choices remain that we are able to make?

Perhaps the choice at least to add an iridescence, like that of our young artist, to our vision and in our experience...?

2.MOSCOW NIGHT GARDEN

I am to stay in the country home of the poet Alexander Zorin.

We come there by dirt road after midnight. There is a high green picket fence . . . and here in the dark is Zorin who takes my hand gently like a child and leads me through the midnight wonder of his garden, which I sense without fully seeing . . . By day it will be huge, chrysanthemums bending over the path, apple and pear trees, holly, tables with cloths under the trees and a high peaked wooden house as if from a fairy tale, painted yellow with blue trim but at night it is all Splendor . . .

Inside it is also so beautiful. He with his wife made it by hand over 25 years and not with great money but with immense beauty. A Korean round lampshade casts patterns of light on the ceiling like a planetarium's stars . . . modern art and icons from Rublev and western sacred art equally but all simple . . .

There are plum blintzes and talk of Rilke, whom Zorin does not think had a coherent spiritual vision although it is amazingly subtle in detail . . . but never breaking through to full realization . . . to "knowing what he knows" (I am paraphrasing a late conversation in Zorin's limited English and my more limited Russian and with a dictionary on the kitchen table between us). He tells me that he was a sailor. He wears, as I remember, always a turtleneck and has a face both soft and hard, a working man's face in one aspect, and yet among the subtlest of faces and he has a telescope and loves to look at the stars.

And on the ceiling, the radiant pattern of a galaxy swirling as the light moves.

X

THE USES OF NOTHING

1.

HAVING THE OPPORTUNITY to listen to a tape made of
the poet Robert Lax by his friend Judith Emery, I was
struck by his saying that for a modern person to be in
a room with Ad Reinhardt's famous Black Paintings all
around is to be as close as we can come to what Medieval people felt in a Cathedral.

Not so very long after that there was an exhibition of
the Black Paintings in New York, and I had that experience and can verify that for me it was to feel in the
presence of the Holy.

I had then been asked to speak to the Merton Society,
and so I started from where I was, and where I knew

Merton had been all the more, and not least through his friendship with Reinhardt, in the place of holy Nothingness, and this is what, in a somewhat different form, I said.

2.

THE, AT LEAST IN SOME MOMENTS, Catholic philosopher Ludwig Wittgenstein provides a good starting for discussing negative or apophatic theology with his famous dictum that "concerning that whereof one cannot speak, thereof one must be silent."

That reserve before the unknowable depth of things is the characteristic of apophatic theology—thought which says only that God is not this and not that, not his attributes, not anything among existent things and therefore beyond even existence as we know it. In contrast to this is positive or kataphatic statement and theology which says that nonetheless it is not wrong understanding and within the limits of our knowledge, to say that God is good, is love, is true, and so on. These two workings of mind typically occur together like inhalation and exhalation of the lungs or the yes / no of our bicameral brains...so we see and experience and say, thank you Lord, "This too is Thou..." and then, but, "Neither is this Thou..."

Charles Williams elucidating expression of apophatic and kataphatic was, "The way of affirmation of images," and, "The way of negation of images." This seems to me helpful.

Now one person by temperament and thought may tend more to the apophatic, negative, and another to the positive. So too with schools of thought, and so for Thomas Merton Buddhism was a sort of radical apophatic theology and his own tendency was towards the apophatic and in this he found reinforcement in the eastern Christian tradition.

May we add that it is not only awareness of the limitation of words but also awareness of emptiness which underlies apophatic thinking. As St. Francis said to Brother Leo, "We have nothing except emptiness of our own to offer God." This sense is also of course explicit in Buddhism, Taoism and so on . . .

A second word of preface might be that in speaking of theology one wants to withdraw from all cleverness of the sort C.S. Lewis recalls in a conversation with two priests who, when he said that everything is created, one said to the other as an aside, "Except the uncreated energies, of course," and they both laughed to Lewis' irritation at their shared knowledge of the term presumably from St Gregory Palamas, which Lewis did not know. There is that temptation with many things and not least perhaps with apophatic theology.

On the contrary, rather than being the movement of intellectual counters for one-upping the other or being a process of refinement by footnotes of a received knowledge, theology must come from living engagement with God. And so it does in Thomas Merton always doesn't it? He used apophasis, negation in theology drawn from many sources including the Christian East as we shall see but for now the starting point I choose is that of Merton's exchange with his friend the painter, Ad Reinhardt, whose own series of Black Paintings move to the ever purer and emptier, the place beyond images as well as words. The black paintings are composed with two superimposed rectangles making a sort of cross as one looks into the black and yet variously nuanced surface. However, the cross glimpsed is not a stopping point; the paintings have no "solution" but shift before the eye. Now Merton had written a jacket blurb for the Catholic artist William Congdon's book *My Disc of Gold.*

Reinhardt in a letter asked Merton in effect if he had taken leave of his taste and senses? In the mannered (rather beat generation) style of their correspondence,

Reinhardt asks, "Have you no respect for sacredness and art? ... Are you throwing in the trowel at long last? Can't you tell your impasto from a holy ground? ... We'll send help, hold on, old man."

To this Merton replied in the same style "Truly immersed in the five *skandhas* and plunged in *avidya*, [the *skandas* are the ultimately illusory elements of the human psyche, *avidya* is illusion.] Merton goes on, "I have taken the shell for the nut and the nut for the nugget and the nugget for the essence and the essence for the such-ness ... I have embraced a bucket of schmaltz." And this is, mannered style aside, a real turning in his orientation.

Perhaps we ought to note that Congdon was not Norman Rockwell, still less a painter of mallard ducks for dentist's waiting rooms, by any stretch. He was an abstract expressionist and remained so after his conversion. What Merton had said in his jacket note to Congdon's book was, "The dynamism of abstraction has been set free from its compulsive, Dionysian and potentially orgiastic self-frustration and raised to the level of spirituality." His Christian work has recognizable figures in the sense that Kandinsky's work contains for example St. George on his horse passing into an almost abstract flow of color.

It is my impression that Reinhardt is arbitrary in setting his own relentless minimalism as the only, or only ideal, way for art. Perhaps Merton's compliance to his friend's thought is a little more than might be necessary for his own way and feeling?

So when a Merton scholar says, "Merton decisively moved to Reinhardt's camp and the world of contemporary art. As an artist, he would not go back to his drawings of Our Lady..." he perhaps simplifies a reality and a turning which is more complex. My own feeling is that whatever his admirations included, Merton's own spirit is as well represented by Congdon's sacred work as by Reinhardt's black paintings.

Nonetheless, personal friendship to Reinhardt aside, this exchange does show the powerful pull of the negative way, the way of rejection of images, on Thomas Merton.

Let us in any case add Reinhardt's words on his Black Paintings in 1962 which Merton used later in a tribute to his friend and which could be used as well to define apophatic theology.

"Separating and defining it more and more, making it purer and emptier, more absolute and more exclusive

—non-objective, non-representational, non-figurative, non-imagist, non-expressionist, non-subjective. The only and one way to say what abstract art or art-as-art is, is to say what it is not..." The drumfire of nons, of negations, to clear the way, reminds of the language of Dionysius, "No shape no form no quality no quantity ... not existent not nonexistent..." The work of Dionysius, a Syrian monk of the 6th century or so, was immensely and variously influential in East and West. Merton knew his work, of course, from many sources, not least St. Thomas, who cited him thousands of times, but also knew it as mediated through the thought of the contemporary Orthodox theologian Vladimir Lossky.

To the side, Reinhardt's words echo not only Dionysius but also St. John of the Cross in paraphrase by T. S. Eliot and set out as a spiritual way:

> To arrive where you are, to get from where
>   you are not,
> You must go by a way wherein there is no
>   ecstasy.
> In order to arrive at what you do not know
> You must go by a way which is the way of
>   ignorance.
> In order to possess what you do not possess
> You must go by the way of dispossession.

In order to arrive at what you are not
You must go through the way in which you
    are not.

And what you do not know is the only thing
    you know
And what you own is what you do not own
And where you are is where you are not.

Now we just mentioned the theologian Vladimir
Lossky, whose seminal book *The Mystical Theology of the
Eastern Church* sets out the negative, apophatic way and
the kataphatic positive on the other hand, and indicates
the apophatic as the deeper and truer way and as central
to Eastern theology. Merton read this in 1950 in French
as a letter to Jean Leclerq shows. Later he would read
Lossky's *Vision of God* and, in French again, his study of
Meister Eckhart. Concerning that, Merton wrote in
1961, "It is fabulously good, not only that but it is for
me personally a book of immense and providential importance because I can see right away that I am in the
middle of the most fundamental intuition of unknow-
ing which was the first source of my faith and which
ever since has been my whole life." And beyond Lossky
as A.M. Allchin has shown, Merton knew a range of
other Eastern Orthodox writers (Berdyaev, Bulgakov,
Evdokimov, Florovsky) Of these Berdyaev's sense of
the *ungrund* the abyss of freedom and emptiness beneath

all things can be for example relevant but this testimonial to the confluence of his own intuition with that of Lossky surely represents an important moment . . .

Now, the work of the artist in making his Black Series is a working of negative theology as a way in our time, making it more than a counter or structural element in the system of theologians . . . So here Merton, even finally on his Asian pilgrimage, and others we have spoken of (Reinhardt painting towards the ultimate end of art, Lax reducing poetic language to its minimum) return to the East the gift of the term "apophatic" now made real in life and in inner journey and struggle . . .

It may even appear as an easy way of spiritual engagement for in one respect nothingness is easy to approach, particularly when starting outside definite belief . . .

So Bellow's Mr Sammler in old age when he picks up Meister Eckhart and so Martin Heidegger in his last days and having returned to the church if indeed he ever left it, discussed the nothingness in Eckhart with a priest friend. So also the poet Wallace Stevens in his journey towards God rests for long in the place of Meister Eckhart's emphasis that while we need "God," "It is not the Deity but a human construct beyond which is that which to us is 'nothing'. God operates, the Deity does not operate…"That which permits the thinking and naming of God is not God Himself… or in Scotus Eriugena's categories beyond that which is uncreated and creates there is that which is neither created nor creator. The experimental film director Stan Brakhage said, "It was in a chapel—the Rothko Chapel in Hocton—that I had a sense of nothing—that drew me out to the very limits of my inner being. That's where I think it all begins—in the sense of the ineffable—and I want that to come through me into my work. I want that appreciation of nothing being everything."

Chuang Tse puts it, "To know how to rest in the unknowable is the summit of knowledge." And that can be more or less the last word on the "way of negation of images," the *via negativa*.

However, not everyone who comes this way is called to stop or to stay at that point… so we spoke of Wallace Stevens, yet Stevens in the end, writing to the priest who baptized him, says that he hopes to see him at such and such a time to resume their conversation or if not they will do so in heaven. So that he did not, as it were, rest in a minimalist sense of nothing as being the whole end of the journey but comes to an affirmation resting on the apophatic.

So perhaps what requires an inner work is to find and know the point where emptiness becomes form, as the Heart of Wisdom Sutra says, where emptiness and form, life and death, complete each other. It is this that Merton reaches out to at the end of *Sign of Jonas*, "Within what was not, I am..."

And in his memory of his experience at 4th and Walnut, Merton remembers seeing the Divine in each of the people around as, "A virginal point (la point *vierge* from Louis Massignon on Al Hallaj) in each a point of pure nothingness which is untouched by sin and illusion, a point of pure truth..." and then goes on into affirmations:

> "This little point of nothingness and of our absolute poverty is the pure glory of God written in us. It is so to speak His name written in us, as our sonship. It is like a pure diamond blazing with the invisible light of heaven. It is in everybody, and if we could see it we would see these billions of points of light coming together in the face and blaze of a sun that would make all the darkness and cruelty of life vanish completely."

Perhaps it is this moving beyond nothingness which leads D.T. Suzuki to say, in Dom Aelred Graham's *Conversations Christian and Buddhist*, that Fr. Merton's "nothing" does not go far enough . . . and perhaps this makes Merton's work related to the art of William Congdon as well as to the later art of Ad Reinhardt.

Does not prayer come into focus as the work of moving into the affirmations without losing the depth which negative theology opened?

Now concerning prayer, obviously Merton wrote a very great deal more than we can even cover in outline. But I would like to touch on two points which relate to our theme. First as to what we might call the psychology of prayer and secondly as to the practice and within that the place of the Jesus Prayer.

In his journals, Thomas Merton has a wonderful passage where he compares one's mind engaged in prayer to a sea with its many levels and currents, there is warmth and coldness, there is a level where the water is moving swiftly, and there are all kinds of sea creatures, and then down to a depth where there is hardly any movement and fish, if any, remote to the surface . . . In prayer one accepts and moves through and somehow integrates all the levels. These are the "multiple states of being" of Rene Guenon . . . or the sense of a human existence as a radius extending from the heart of things to the very edge. It is apparent that we ourselves are formed of being and nothingness.

A form of prayer that gathers up levels of being and focuses them is what is often called centering prayer, the use of a mantra in effect. In the Eastern Church this often means the prayer repeating the name of Jesus and the systematic practice of which is called Hesychasm. We know that Merton lectured with enthusiasm on this practice to the monks, and Mr. Jonathan Moltaldo has put together a set of marginal notes and underlinings made by Merton in his copy of the compilation *The Art of Prayer,* and particularly in the writings of Theophan the Recluse. One in caps, "It is time for you to learn more perfectly how to remain within [and] abandon external plans." To this of course a number of references to the Jesus Prayer in his various writings. Remaining within our emphasis on prayer grounded in the awareness of "nothing" let me give what seems to me an excellent example of this working in the minimal poetry of his friend Robert Lax: the poem *One Stone*, which begins:

> "one stone one stone one stone
> i lift one stone one stone
> i lift one stone and i am thinking..."

and continues the repetitive sense of the careful action . . . surely with prayer in the I am thinking, or
rather, if the thinking is not a verbal prayer, in its attention it passes into prayer. This is the work of turning
the apophatic to a point beyond itself.

I would like to propose in fact that it is the flow of
prayer which is the ground and perhaps the key to the
understanding of Lax's later work. In this differentiated
somewhat from the relentless minimalism of the late
work of Samuel Beckett.

Now in and beyond prayer, surely it requires a resurrection to say in the words of the *Upanishad* "I know
the great One who is beyond the darkness in knowledge of whom alone one passes death . . ." In what
measure the Resurrectional synthesis is achieved in
Merton, in Lax, in Reinhardt, and we might add Henri
LeSaux and Dom Bede and of course many others, is
a matter of the inner life of each but what we may say
is that their work, and the work of Thomas Merton, is
a moving towards the holding together of what is not
and what is . . .

Dom Bede Griffiths working within Indian spirituality
says that it is the cross and the Resurrection alone,
which dispel all illusion.

Within the Eastern Church in our day Simeon Frank suggests another approach or aspect of synthesis, writes on "not-God" as within God—seeming to overcome the line between what is and was and what might have been or is not... but this is beyond our scope here.

I suppose the burning bush which burns without being consumed in the Old Testament or the chalice, then the Holy Grail of the medieval cycle, represent this point of the presence and endurance of a separate world of creation founded on the emptiness and void but it is also first of all as Dom Bede Griffith's puts it the death and Resurrection of Jesus Christ which joins the negative and the positive and all the dualities...

For one summation we might say for Merton in the words concluding the *Prajnaparamita Sutra*, that "great mantra which dispels all fear"—"*Gyate gyate para sam gyate Bodhi Svaha!* (Gone gone beyond gone utterly beyond. Oh what an Awakening! All Hail!)"

The waking of Resurrection morning and so no schematic end, only Resurrection in words of Jacob Boehme, "My triumphing can be compared to nothing but the experience in which life is generated in the midst of death or like the resurrection from the dead."

And as Fr. Alexander Men said in his last public words: "The victory which began at Easter will continue as long as the worlds endure..."

But let us add again that resurrection life is in all true life and the resolution of all that seems unresolved and even unresolvable is within the experience of that life and accessible to us by example in the work of people like Thomas Merton, but also of course in our own experience.

3.

SINCE THAT LECTURE I have found and read in, what I had not read during my years in Japan, the work of the so called "Kyoto School" of philosophy; in Kitaro Nishida and Keiji Nishitani in particular and in Fr. James Heisig's magisterial study *Philosophers of Nothingness*. The work of these men, and Hajime Tanabe also of that school, is an amazing attempt to find a global standpoint in religious thought by men who were Buddhists but felt that they could articulate their thought fully in terms of western philosophy and even in Christian terms using, in particular, the Kenosis, the self-emptying of Christ. It is in the negation of ourselves that we come closest to God, who is also the one who negates Himself. Both God and man come into being through nothingness and self-negation.

It is my feeling that this can be very true and it has been the subject of our thoughts on Reinhardt and Merton and Lax, and yet there is a certain reality beside this of the permanence, and indeed immortality, of the soul. Kafka's "the Imperishable." We have represented this immortality in speaking of the Angelicals as a dimension of humanity which links us into the Eternal.

For the Christian perhaps the language of nothingness on the one hand, and the language of affirmation both seem appropriate and somehow necessary, and their synthesis must be in experience. Here we are at one with the Kyoto School, though for the Christian the Resurrection will more easily and immediately be the focal point.

Thomas Merton expresses it this way:

> "Man follows the Risen Savior through the tomb and the hell in the center of his own being to emerge to the heaven which is the heart of his own nothingness."

XI

FOUR

1. WRITING

I heard recently of a devout old Archbishop of New York, whom I had met in my youth, that one evening a visitor came upon him reclining with his hand moving in the air. "You must think I am cuckoo," said the Archbishop, "but this is the way I write poetry at night."

It seems that he did write rather many, mostly unpublished surely and perhaps all now forgotten, but how, then, how could the movement of a hand in the air be transcribed?

"He had his own special view of the world, his own themes. He wrote poems, maybe not very good ones, but at heart he was truly a poet. A poet is first of all,

someone who sees the world in a different way, some-
one who has his own secret theme." Fr. Alexander
Schmemann, remembering Metropolitan Leonty
Turkevich.

2. AS IF

Sergei Fudel, a Russian layman (1900–1977) who was
imprisoned three times for his faith and who died in
exile, wrote,

> In the hymns to St Sergius of Radonezh we say
> that 'he lived his bodily life spiritually, spent his
> days on earth as if it were heaven, communed
> with people as if they were angels, and his own
> world was otherworldly.' perhaps we do not
> want to live like this but each of us must try,
> within the measure of his strength . . .

Is not the "as if" the key? By that a world is created
which mirrors heaven and yet is not a different place
from the every-day world of brute factuality, though it
is the deep reality of that world. His disciples said to
him, "When will the new world come?" He said to
them, "What you are looking forward to has come, but
you don't know it." Gospel of Thomas 51.

3. BOUNDARIES

The crossing of boundaries is not a one-time thing, or an occasional thing, but a permanent widening of one's heart and mind in realizing the lack of borders between people and destinies, which is also the full meaning of Christ's Incarnation.

This sharing and softening of boundaries must not be balanced by a strengthening of some other boundary on the other side...by a balancing divisiveness... Identity with the poor does not mean class anger against the rich, learning as an Eastern Orthodox to appreciate the Catholics does not mean a balancing, "but we both can be happy that we are not Baptists."

To learn to feel oneself at home in the world, almost without barrier between self and world, by a lake at sunset with the only sound the stirring of wind over water does not mean to feel, "How foolish it is to enjoy bright lights and partying, how vain it is to be with people, they tire me so..."

4. BREAD

"In my way of thinking meaning is caught like a slice of light through prismed glass and then let go as another color comes forward . . . yet the moments joined by a gravity of intention . . ."

This from a letter from Steven Kozler, a priest who died early in his ministry, suddenly and while making bread for the altar.

In this letter written, it seems, the day before his death, he went on to speak of the joy, after for a time trying to tailor his thought and prayer to the ways of a simple and linear theology and pattern, of returning to this, to him, natural and unified vision which he represents by a picture drawn from a visit to Japan:

"I remember the rice fields and how only the ever in and out drone of the cicadas clothed the glorious silent space of the mountain fields"

XII

ST. NIKOLAI KASATKIN AND FR. ALEXANDER MEN ON WORLD RELIGIONS

A Lecture Given at Chevetogne

I was in Japan when Nikolai Kasatkin was recognized as a saint and as founder of the Japanese Orthodox Church given the title "equal of the apostles." I wished to know him as well as possible and so I set myself the task of translating his sermons, which were written in the Japanese of 100 years ago, as remote from modern Japanese perhaps as Slavonic is from Russian, so much has that language changed. So the Orthodox priest's sermon can sometimes be mostly the explanation of the meaning of the text of the Gospel from the old language, somehow perhaps an Orthodox situation? Anyway it is also so in Japan. But gradually I filled a notebook with these sermons deciphered as if from a

code and I was struck by the figure of this man ... First
by his titanic will, a true soldier, or samurai, of Christ
living in considerable isolation for 50 years and yet
building a national church. Beyond this at many points
I was struck by his pastoral spirit—how he reached out
to the Japanese trying to find the words they could receive, making adjustments (of the date of Christmas
into December so that they could celebrate the New
Year) and when there was war with Russia, telling
them to pray for the victory of their nation.

Fr. Alexander Men, as we are gathered to consider, was
a great pastor in his very different circumstance. There
is however, different though the circumstances of Japan
in 1900 and Russia in our times, one point at least
where their pastoral visions can be said to overlap and
that is where I should like to share some words from
one of St. Nikolai's sermons.

Fr. Men wrote a six-volume history of world religions
showing how all are part of God's guiding of the world
to the encounter with Christ. "Everything that rises
must converge," as Fr. Teilhard de Chardin said.

St Nikolai, with less study in world religions and less
reading, nonetheless out of the pastoral need to explain
to Japanese believers how Christianity could fit to the

history and culture of their country came to a similar vision of things which he began to develop from his first encounters with Buddhism, staying for some time in a Buddhist temple in Tokyo while the Holy Ressurection Cathederal was being built. His first encounters with the native religion, Shinto, had been less positive, being threatened with death by a young Shintoist whom however, impressed by Nikolai's courage and calm, became a convert and the first Orthodox Japanese priest. And Nikolai saw good also in the Shinto heritage.

Later I will return to the consideration of the significance of Fr. Men's work on world religion but first I should like to lay out in some detail, and as a basis, an outline of a key writing by St. Nikolai on this.

He expresses his experience of and evaluation of Japanese religion in a long letter of report to the Holy Synod in Moscow but also he expresses the essence of all of this simply but clearly in the sermon "The True Religion and the Ethics of the World" which he gave at the Tokyo Cathedral to seminarians on Holy Thursday 1910.

He begins by considering the missionary situation. "In our world here and today there are of course those who

say that in this Japan we have had fine morals since ancient times so the religion from foreign lands is unnec-
essary. However we also are fully aware of Japan's fine
ethics . . . Japan has the very finest. Shinto with its purity
and honesty, Buddhism with its mercy and compassion,
and Confucianism which instills Justice and love."

However all these things are finally related to the world
of action and are in themselves not the full Word "of
the heavenly Father and of the human soul." Buddhism
and the other religions are "like nursemaids who have
brought up this Japanese nation until now but have not
power to bring them to the heavenly Father." Because
of these old faiths, Japan has a high morality and a people of good character and "they have received great
grace and in an age when any number of nations have
fallen Japan has endured over all the centuries since its
foundation . . . this is surely the protection of God answering to this people's virtue." And it is also a grace of
God that the true teaching has entered this country
. . . and the land will be still more blessed."

It is always a mistake to say that because one has ethics
one needs no further knowledge of truth. Imagine, he
goes on, a village whose good reputation the Emperor
hears and invites them to come and visit his palace, and
they say "we need no good beyond that of our village."

This is the provincialism of those who say that they do not need to hear of Christ although their teaching, Buddhism and Confucianism "originally proceeds from God and Buddha and Confucius did no more than tell what is engraved in the heart." Natural religion is in itself incomplete . . . "to preach Christianity and introduce this people to the Heavenly Father is to bring ever greater blessedness to this Japanese nation."

Some doubt the idea of divine miracles in history or intervention but, "As we are living in this world we are always and everywhere within a miracle of God . . . this world is entirely miraculous . . ." This is, in summary, St. Nikolai's sermon.

We would note that St. Nikolai does not engage what could be said to be a deeper metaphysics of Buddhism, for example the sense of "Nothingness" and "Void" as later Christian writers will do. Nonetheless his orientation of in a sense full acceptance is in the spirit of the early Christian Fathers who regarded Greek and other cultures as being, like the Hebrew Old Testament, a good to be accepted as the ground which is completed in Christ. The phrase Nikolai uses of "nursemaid" is an early Christian expression for previous philosophy and religion.

Without then a direct connection to the work of Fr. Alexander Men perhaps we could say that the vision of St. Nikolai Kasatkin, born out of the pastoral situation in Japan, both reaches back to the vision of the early church fathers such as St. Justin who said that all that is good is the heritage of Christians, whatever its source, and unites to and supports the vision of the world moving through the ages to God which was in Fr. Men's work on religions and at the heart of his pastoral work also.

So for one thing we see Fr. Men as in the tradition of St. Stephen of Perm, St. Innokenty Venniaminov and here clearly St. Nikolai Kasatkin, in openness to the cultures of those we approach in mission, and as to other religions the case is explicit in St. Nikolai. first of all to restore an orientation to the world of faith for Russians.

But I think there is something further. The volumes on world religions by Fr. Men were of course intended not for Buddhists and Hindus and Muslims but for a Russian people made largely secular and separated from all religious knowledge by the long period of oppression of all faith. So the purpose of the work was first of all to restore an orientation to the world of faith to all Russians.

However in the future I could forsee a further importance of Fr. Alexander's work being realized—that it is a building of bridges to other families of humanity and their faith. This is in accord with the example of early Christians such as St. Justin who said that all that is good in human culture is our inheritance in Christ, and it is explicitly stated by St. Nikolai as we have seen, but it is a work of bridge building which has hardly begun and in which Fr. Men's work can perhaps come to seem an early and significant accomplishment within this work.

Fr. Raimundo Pannikar of India said, "Christ is the bridge where Christianity and Hinduism meet." This is also the Christocentric openness of Fr. Alexander Men, the realization that we are completed in all of the others, and they are completed in us, and we and they and all things are completed in Christ . . . the Christ who fills the future as Fr. Teilhard spoke so well of or as in Boris Pasternak's poem of the centuries coming to Christ like barges on the river of time . . .

This vision which is in Fr. Alexander Men of convergence of faith can open out perhaps a new dimension of importance to his work on world religion, as it extends the work of St. Nikolai and others before him.

XIII

SHIMMERING

OUR KNOWLEDGE INDEED PASSES between affirming and negating, in part because of our bicameral brains no doubt, but also because we stand, as St. Philaret said, on a "bridge of diamond" between the infinite and the nonexistent. We see then always with these two eyes and have, as it were, a shimmering knowledge of reality. I started to write on prayer starting from this quality of our experience and here are two sections of that reflection.

1. TRUE THOMAS

Thomas Rymer, a poet, or more precisely, a character in a poem of fifteenth-century Scotland, met a "lady bright" dressed all in green who showed him a "fair road winding through ferny fields".. It was a road he had not seen before; had it been there before he met the lady? It seems to be somehow between the two roads he knew. "Thither you and I must go," she says and, as in a dream, he rides with her out of his world. For on that road they soon pass beyond the light of sun or moon but the sea is near and they hear the beating of the surf, the ever-alternating roar and hiss of the coming and going of the waves...

They have found a road which has its great perils... Putting it in terms of our own experience we may say that God must be always in view, always affirming for God's sake, negating for God's sake, or else through the shimmering all that will appear will be the path to the twilight land of faery, or in "demythologized" terms, to the place where everything is possible because nothing is certain, one may suppose anything but know nothing.

I think that the old writers such as Thomas Rymer saw at once the way and its mysterious attractiveness, on the one hand, and its danger if God is not always in mind, on the other, and without really sorting it out represent both by the Faery realm.

And the amazing writer, Ibn al'Arabi, of twelfth-century Seville, author of a body of theological work as large as an encyclopedia and yet no drudge but a man with a burning heart and eye, found in his scriptures the words that God Most High, "Gave to man two eyes as he set before him two roads." These are the ways of affirmation and negation, of yes and no, and he says that most men, indeed even most godly and spiritual men, use only one or the other or one and then the other. But he says the best vision is that of both eyes at once. Then one sees a path in which both ways are joined in one.

"'Listen! It's music—like voices calling, and bells of ice! And look—there's the Old Straight Track!' Suddenly through the hills and over the...hill a Shimmering line...flowed, silver...glistening, alive." *The Moon of Gomrath*, Alan Garner.

The nostalgia for a third way, beyond the ways of right and left that we know, the yes and no of the bicameral brain, lies behind the search for "the old straight roads" by which it is said ancient man connected his holy places along lines following the straight contours, or "ley-lines," of the earth itself. The 19th-century, self-taught and romantic archeologist Alfred Watkins trekked all over Britain tracing straight lines between mounds, and towers, and towns. It was a somewhat "sub-defined" research, as he says, "In field work, remember that if evidence were plentiful and easy to find, ley-lines would have been discovered long ago . . ." And, "Faint traces of ancient track are most easily seen when the sun is low on one side—in late evening . . ." But even if a straight path reveals itself in the glimmering twilight, there remains at least the problem with this, which J. R. R. Tolkien sensibly suggests, that since the world is round there are no true straight lines, all lines bend and return to their point of origin and space itself (Einstein showed) is curved back on itself. But he allows that for the faeries, or elves, it is still possible to find the "straight road" that does not bend and so rises beyond our world as the world below curves and recedes away into darkness.

But a road that was straight in that absolute sense, would surely in a curved space, appear to waver and shimmer . . . So also integral knowledge would shimmer between affirmation and denial.

Perhaps this, and not just the twilight path of speculation, is what Thomas Rymer found, for now he has a coat and shoes "of velvet green" and, more important, he is unable to say anything but truth and is forever known as "True Thomas."

2. KENJI

As a young priest in a country town in Northern Japan, I spent the long snowbound winter evenings translating *Night of the Milky Way Railroad*, by Kenji Miyazawa. Miyazawa was a writer of the 1920s and 1930s and one of the Renaissance men of that period of cultural change. He was an educator, agricultural reformer, scientist, religious thinker (a lay leader of the Jodo Shin sect of Buddhism), and in all a diverse man deeply proud of his roots in the northern countryside and of its simple manners and speech. This book is a story of a boy, Kenji, who finds himself riding on a train, with a friend, through the stars. He is living, and (though Kenji does not then know it) his friend has died, yet they are to share this journey. They see many things both ordinary and strange, and there are a great many reflecting signs:

> Here and there in the field stood phosphorescent reflecting signals. The distant ones were small, the nearer ones larger. The far-off signs were bright orange or yellow and clearly visible, while the closer signs were a shimmering blue or white. The signals, triangular or square or zigzag like lightning, or formed like chains

aligned in various ways, filled the field with blinking light...

A ride on one of the country local lines of northern Japan is a special experience even when the train does not leap the track and wander among the stars. It is a meandering journey with meals taken from wooden lunch boxes and packs of oranges whose peels are strewn on the coach floor. The train passes through a mountain tunnel, for the interior of Japan is all mountain country, and emerges into some bright valley with thatch-roofed farm houses nestled in the midst of rice fields. Drying fruit hangs from their eaves and thin pencils of smoke rise from their chimneys into the morning air, and there is a small island of woodland with a bright red shrine gate at its margin, and there is a bright little river with a shimmering of fractured light along its flow, and there... but now the train enters another tunnel and as that brightness came out of the darkness, now again shadow displaces light, and then suddenly it is day again but a completely new scene: of forest with high filtered light through the pines...

So I remember, and so also the mood of the two boys on the Milky Way train shifts from moment to moment and scene to scene. From laughter to tears to thoughtfulness in the change of instants. So it is with children and not only with children, for we too find light and darkness passing over our faces as quickly as the blinking of a railroad signal...

Later Kenji finds himself back by a river running through his home town, in which the river of the stars above is reflected, his friend is gone but beside him is one of his teachers who explains something to the shaken and distraught boy:

> Look here! take a hold of yourself! Try to see things as I do just a little alright? And he raised a finger and slowly lowered it. All at once Kenji felt himself and his thoughts and the train and the teacher and the heavenly river of the Milky Way and everything coming together in a radiant flash. Then, silently, it was gone. Flash! it lit up and was extinguished. And when lit up, the whole wide world opened out, and all history with it in that flash. Softly it died out into emptiness and that was all. The flashes came at faster intervals—and then, very soon after, Kenji found everything just as it had been before. 'How's that? So you see Kenji your experiment in life will have to include both the beginning

and the end of this our disjointed thought process. And that is a difficult thing! But of course it's alright to limit yourself to the thought of a single moment...

Lately rereading this part of the old translation, I have begun to understand something perhaps. When I first worked on it, those many years ago, it seemed to me that the teacher's words and induced vision concerning the pulsing quality of things was simply a matter of some Buddhist sense of the transitory nature of reality—the world appears and disappears and another rises, off and on like a blinker light.

But now the words stop me, like a reflecting sign, and I see that it is about the process of thought itself and about our vision of every moment, which contains both affirmation and negation, silence and word, emptiness and form. So where I had mistakenly rendered the teacher's words that "your... experiment... may be limited to a single time." (as of a period or phase of history) I now find, "... to the thought of a single moment."

The pulse, the shimmering, is there in the heart of the moment, every moment contains its end and negation, just as our every word is grounded in silence. The teacher's words to Kenji are, within the context of the book, initiatory and perhaps they may begin for us an initiation of the understanding which we seek in relation to that special movement of mind which is prayer...

Now the theologians know "positive" and "negative" theology, the kataphatic and apophatic of Dionysius, and the two ways are regarded generally as discrete ways to be chosen, which we might call "the way of affirmation of images" and "the way of negation of images." The first way says, "This too is Thou!" and makes the affirmation of the world for God's sake. The second way says, "Neither is this Thou!" and makes the negation also for God's sake. So it is suggested that the choice of ways may be a matter of spiritual temperament. Or rather, that both are tools to be used in their appropriate times, while one may more naturally and regularly incline to one or the other.

Yet both are grounded in the experience of every moment, in the inhaled breath and in the pulsing rhythm of the blood...

XIV

ACAUSALITY, SPIRIT, AND FREEDOM

THIS AGAIN IS AN ESSAY that I gave in slightly different form as a paper which I read at a conference organized by St. Philaret's Institute in Moscow.

THE TOPIC OF COINCIDENCE, of the significant relationship of seemingly random events, is certainly a primary religious subject. For one thing it represents the Providential in our experience of life. It is also a subject which is pressed on our consideration by developments in our time. For example the discovery of the 'indeterminate' movement of sub-atomic particles by modern physics, and in particular by Werner von Heisenberg, seems to put chance at the very basis of the material world. And in the field of psychology there is the theory of "synchronicity" announced by Dr. Carl G. Jung, with supporting work by the physicist Wolfgang Pauli. "Synchronicity," which Jung defines as a principle of "a-causal connection" of events, brings into the field of psychology and daily life that same mysterious vision of the world which quantum physics opens to us in the subatomic realm.

However, this whole subject of the relation of events in our life, apparently random yet mysteriously connected, has not, unless I am mistaken, been discussed very deeply by theological writers—either as to the significance of "Providence," or as to the understandings of modern physics and psychology. I do not know why this is, unless it be related to the hesitance of theologians to touch on questions of personal spiritual experience. The number of excellent books on prayer in our century is perhaps not more than a very few, I think of Anthony Bloom, C.S. Lewis's *Letters to Malcolm*, of Romano Guardini's little book on prayer, perhaps you will think of others, but they are in any case not many. And this whole area of coincidence and random event seems if possible more delicate and difficult for theologians to approach.

I believe that this reticence in relation to personal experience is deeply unfortunate, and I would like to make a, of course, very modest venture into this field.

Before, however, continuing the meditation of the question of the appearance of pattern in apparently unrelated events, that is to say the problem as it presents itself to us today, I should like to start with some background in the Patristic period.

St Gregory of Nyssa's *Contra Fatum* (*Against Determinism*) is perhaps as good an example of the way the matter appeared to the Church Fathers as we will find. Gregory is writing specifically against the supposed determination of life by the stars, astrology. Astrology had an honored role in the ancient world, well; even the three Magi who came to Bethlehem were practitioners of that science. The great philosopher Plotinus said that for everything in the world the stars represented the determined order of things, but that the spirit could escape to a place of unity with God beyond determination.

This is one possible solution. But Gregory seeks another. First he recognizes that there is a Divine harmony and pattern in all things which is reflected in human nature. "The entire world is a kind of musical harmony whose artisan is God [and] in man's nature all the music of the universe is seen ... as the whole is contained in the particular ..."

So far, in fact, Gregory is in agreement with the astrologers and old philosophers, but then he goes on that at the root of everything is freedom, "So that the good might be present in our lives, not by involuntary determinism, but by our free choice."

But if there is a universal pattern and harmony, in the world and in humanity, how can there be at the same time freedom? Gregory does not pursue this question (content to point out the contradictions of astrological ideas) but it seems to me that the contemporary question of synchronicity, of random events, both in physics and in our experience, challenges us to continue his analysis a little further. I will do so, if I may, with a series of brief sections (perhaps something like the "century" form used by St. Maximus and others, but I will not offer a hundred, only fifteen in keeping with our time and my possibilities) However this form allows for a looser relation of thought which yet creates finally a pattern, rather as the apparently random events we are discussing form the mysterious pattern of our life.

It is like the movement of a butterfly's flight maybe, but then the poet Yeats said, "Wisdom is a butterfly and not a gloomy bird of prey."

So let us begin our little butterfly flight . . .

1. THE COINCIDENCE OF EVENTS in one aspect is "Providence," or in secular terms "good luck," but in another aspect coincidence is the projected fears of the nervous seeing threatening patterns where there are none. Both these perceptions are a personalization of the way we see the world, but the one is above our average experience of life as neutral events, and the other is below it.

2. IF WE OPEN THE BIBLE at random and find a verse absolutely appropriate to the need of the moment, or find suddenly in a book or newspaper something exactly relevant to the moment, this is an example of what Jung meant by "synchronicity." The whole system of the old Chinese classic the *I Ching* depends on this finding of meaning in random reading.

3. FILL A PAGE WITH DOTS evenly distributed and then draw a pattern connecting them . . . perhaps a circle . . . or a star of David . . . was the pattern in the dots as implicit in them, or is it purely arbitrary to find this pattern?

4. JOHN CORNWELL, a journalist author, in an interesting book about apparent supernatural events within the churches today, *The Hiding Places of God*, notes that at moments when we are beginning to move towards God, the appearance of significant coincidence seems to be more frequent.

5. CONNECTIONS, HOWEVER, can be made by an alertness of physical observation, which appears as psychic intuition. For example of body posture or tone of voice, etc., which the mind processes subconsciously and comes to an apparent intuition about the person one is speaking to.

Sherlock Holmes to Watson on first meeting, "I perceive you are just returned from Afghanistan." A priest hearing confession or a psychiatrist will, when alert, be listening for all these nonverbal signs and perhaps for others beyond the ordinary sensory range.

6. A SUNFLOWER IN THE FIELD, or blazing in a painting by Van Gogh, reminds of the sun. So does gold, and the radiance of silver suggests the secondary light of the moon. The Florentine priest Marsilio Ficino, in *The Book of Life*, uses such correspondences as basis of a system of medication. In one aspect this (and homeopathy in general) is an operation of magic. But we come again to the question of whether a pattern drawn connecting the dots is or can become in some way more than an illusion.

7. THE NERVOUS IMAGINATION organizes events also of course in patterns more or less bizarre and yet meaningful, often fearfully so, but sometimes hopefully so, to the viewer... A friend had a period of suddenly noticing the color green everywhere and the word green etc.... This was a fairly benign illusory effect (since in fact green is everywhere) and passed. On another hand, begin to fear some disease and you may be surprised how often you hear it mentioned, etc.

8. A PHOTOGRAPHER ISOLATING AND FIXING a place and moment in the field of what we see makes it somehow symbolic and deeply resonant. Now it is not illusion, but heightened reality which is offered to us.

Perhaps the eye of simplicity, what St. Ephrem of Syria calls "the luminous eye," can enable us to see the world in this way. The eye of the saint like the eye of the artist or poet.

9. "WHERE SHALL I GO FROM THY SPIRIT? If I take the wings of the morning and dwell in the uttermost part of the sea, even there [the presence and purpose of God.]" So the problem of continual prayer is not so much to pray; really we pray, that is to say we interact with God, in all the thoughts and acts of all our days, but the problem is to know that we are praying. By so knowing and resting in that knowing our life becomes prayer that is consciously offered, and in that offering is our peace.

10. SO IF THE NERVOUS IMAGINATION detects a foolish or malevolent organization of things, a truer vision—a seeing of what we see and knowing of what we know—sees events as flowing from God like leaves of some tree whose roots are far above us...

11. I THINK THIS AWARENESS, the true awareness of Divine pattern, is given in the Holy Spirit as a sort of gift.

Though it is not one of the gifts mentioned explicitly by St. Paul, we might relate it to the "word of wisdom" or "knowledge," and like all gifts it is to be received and used. By so receiving as a gift of God the awareness of pattern, we are protected from the dark side of vision of synchronicity—fearfulness on the one hand or making much of oneself on the other hand, for clinically paranoia and megalomania go together. As received in God the sense of pattern has the lightness of awareness that the pattern is not inherent in oneself.

12. SURELY ALL OF US HAVE EXPERIENCE both of that dark organization of things which falls below everyday reality and which is untrue, and of that true sense of pattern which is above and behind it. For the nervous, the way forward is not so much in a deadening of the psychic sense, but as for all of us (and the nervous is in degree all of us) in humility, lightness, inner freedom, that freedom which is the gift only of Pentecost.

13. THANKS TO GOD who makes all things to be Signs of His Glory... and in moments and in a flash allows us to read the language, or at least to conceive the al-

phabet, of Grace and to see the words beneath the
stones in the river and to perceive the diagram of the
Glory.

14. THE HOLY SPIRIT is the "a-causal connecting principle" A-causal because the Spirit is free and so the connections are there not in necessity but only in
freedom...which is to say, that are and are not
there...are there only to freedom...and yet again the
pattern merges into the ground..."form is emptiness
and emptiness is form" as the *Heart Sutra* says...but for
emptiness may we not now read "Glory?"

15. IN JOHN 17, that deepest of all human writings as
it seems to me (regarded, that is, as a document)
"Glory" is used to signify the "Holy Spirit."The Spirit
is then both Connectivity and Ground..and the joy of
seeing the connectivity is really in seeing the Ground
of all in the Glory.

SO HERE AT THE END we come to the same point as
Gregory did answering the problematics of his time,
but perhaps in meeting the questions of our own time

we are led to formulate a little further that mystery of the human person and of freedom and of the Spirit. I cannot say that we have achieved that in these brief words, but perhaps at least we have pointed the way towards that further opening of the mystery of the person . . . And in so doing, again, indicated the ground of all in Spirit and Glory.

XV

SAVING THE EXCLUDED MIDDLE

THERE ARE TWO CONTRASTING Japanese sayings concerning spirituality. One, "Enter through the form," implies that right practice of an art or spiritual discipline comes first and then the acquisition of the inwardness of the thing. The other, "A direct transmission outside all scriptures and pointed straight to the heart," suggests the opposite.

A Vermeer painting of a young woman with a water jug, or playing a lute, or practicing the piano seems to epitomize the first dictum, as being all form and surface. Rembrandt's *Prodigal Son* goes immediately to the heart through every aspect of its working.

In logic "the law of the excluded middle" is that a proposition must be true or false. If we say that the Church is an historical institution, or if we say that the Church is a mystical rather than sociological or historical reality, we are expressing two different views. On the one hand they do not logically make an either/or division rather than a both/and one, but on the other hand, most people seem to move so strongly to the one or the other pole as to virtually exclude the other.

In his pages on "The idea of the Church," in his book *God With Us*, the Russian Orthodox philosopher Simeon Frank gives what seems to me a deeper and truer view. Frank says that there is, "An inherent duality in the realization of faith," and, hence, there are two aspects to the essential unity of the Church, that of an historical and human institution embodying its reality, and that of a reality whose shape and limits are undefinable and unknowable. These two aspects need each other to be true...

However, also they have a complex relation of coincidence and solidarity, and also of inevitable difference and opposition. Naturally—but Frank would say wrongly—people tend to subsume the mystical in the solidarity or subsume the institutional Church to the mystical and universal. One needs to feel and live with both the nearness and the distance, the solidarity and the conflict. He goes on to say that Christ left the seeds which rightly became the institution of the Church, but he founded a Divine-human reality, both visible form and invisible essence, not first of an institution isolatable from the rest of reality.

As I look around the Church I find that there are of course a good many people who intuitively come to something like this feeling and for them perhaps Frank's clarity of expression can serve to clarify this. I also see people who lean very strongly and almost exclusively to one pole or the other and either make little of the Church and the sacraments or, on the other hand, tend to see the Church as fully expressed and contained within the concrete historical phenomenon. Yet, with Frank, we must hope for a deepening self-awareness of the Church that in fact finds its base both within and without history.

Is it not the case as we look at Vermeer and Rembrandt who might represent the primacy of form or of inwardness, that in the one artist the Form and in the other the inner message, appear equally as, in Goethe's expression, "deeds of light"?

This light shines perhaps ever most brightly in what would be the "excluded middle," and reconciles, only in itself, the opposites which otherwise have no resolution beyond dialogue and tension.

XVI

TWO APPLE ORCHARDS

THE APPLES ARE GONE NOW from the tree out front
... These orchards from other years and other
places ... The tree here today standing between the sea-
sons. Those trees which seem in memory to suggest not
only the past but also the future.

1.BUTOVO: APPLES FALLING FROM THE PAST

In the afternoon we travel from Moscow to Butovo a
place to the south of Moscow which was a killing
ground used by the Communists for people from the
Moscow area, and in particular in 1937 and 1938.

On the way a lady speaks of Fr. Pavel Florensky's scientific work on seawater during the days before his execution in the northern Solovki camp, and of his intention to do a second volume of *Pillar and Ground of Truth,* this time focused on humanity, as the first is on God. Since we do not have it, drafts were destroyed, we do not know what the final position of his thought was. Then she says we are getting near Butovo and she wishes to be silent for these moments.

There is a new church and a bell tower and there are stones with the inscriptions of many names of those murdered here. In the church the attendants tell us that the names of 10,000 are known but countless others unknown. Included are 900 bishops and priests. Enough record remains of them, that 250 of the 10,000 here have been formally recognized as saints by the Church. 10,000 in the Moscow region in 1937-1938 in just this one place. Think of the whole land and of the whole Communist period.

But we will remember also the day when they will return, and all our mothers and fathers and brothers and sisters and ourselves also will return. I think of Peter de Vries, who wrote, "The recognition of how long, how very long, is the mourners' bench upon which we sit, arms linked in undeluded friendship—all of us, brief links ourselves, in the eternal pity," and so it is not wrong that there are flowers and apple trees also even, beside a mourners bench long enough to stretch to Eden where there were also apples and flowers, or perhaps, indeed, it must be the same garden because it will return. Will return and has returned. We walk in the apple orchard, and there are flowers now and apples on the trees. When we leave, ladies from the church follow us to the gate with a big plate of apples newly fallen, and we eat them in the car. Someone says, "Every centimeter of this place is soaked with blood... eating these apples is like communion."

2. KRAKOW: APPLES FALLING FROM THE FUTURE

Now we have come to the chalet-like retreat center of Andrej and Samita on a hillside near the ancient Polish city of Krakow. Here we will spend the night. It is a good place with apple trees everywhere and I know I must be deeply feeling it a good place because I feel the desire to climb the trees, as when a boy. We sit around a table under the trees, and there is nothing lacking, and the apples are falling continually. This year there are more than ever, it seems, now one falls, now three but it almost seems they are growing faster than falling and how perfect and round they are and how fine the taste... and there is watermelon and coffee too and talk about interior monasticism... and Andrej says... we must open ourselves to God who is coming not from the past but from the future... apples falling like cherry blossoms into, or rather from, a future momentarily at least made present in love and peace.

And under the apple trees Anika played the guitar and sang beneath the weaving branches.

The next morning we spread a cloth on a table in the middle of the orchard and in the early bright light do our service of shared bread and wine... Apples falling still... some great joyful mystery in these ripening and falling apples somehow offering themselves as we offer all things as best we can... and again the growth seeming to more than keep pace with the falling... a circulation of heaven and earth. Our host Andrej says in conversation after that there is much writing about Spirit, about the Holy Spirit, about Pneumatology as it is called, but this is to make it an abstraction and an object not the subject, not the One who acts... what is needed he said is "Pneumatics," the seeing of the Spirit's operation in persons and in the world...

XVII

PIPER

PERHAPS THE FINEST WRITING of *The Wind in the Willows* is in the chapter "Piper at the Gates of Dawn," in which Ratty and Mole hear the music of Creation itself at a magical moment between night and sunrise on the river. Ratty has much better ears than poor mole and tries to convey what he is hearing:

> O Mole! the beauty of it! The merry bubble and joy, the thin clear happy call! Such music I have never dreamed of, and the call in it is stronger than the music is sweet! Row on Mole, row! For the music and call must be for us.

And they come to the place of the music, and the divine

being who is playing the pipes, and now although he cannot hear much, Mole feels,

> ...a great Awe...that turned his muscles to water, bowed his head and rooted his feet to the ground. It was no panic terror—indeed he felt wonderfully at peace and happy—but it was an awe that held him and, without seeing, he knew that it could only mean that some august Presence was very, very near... [and] The two animals, crouching to the earth, bowed their heads and did worship.

After they will forget, the two small creatures as we also do, almost everything they have seen and experienced and known at that break of day on the river. Perhaps it is better, thinks Ratty, as it grows dim in his little mind, "...for it roused a longing in me which is pain."

Having forgotten what they knew, the Rat and the Mole rest on their oars, tired from having been out all night, and now it is day, and then they (or more Ratty whose hearing is better) hear a sound of the wind in the reeds which is like music and the music like something heard before, beautiful beyond words. Now Ratty seems to hear words, words of truth and comfort and peace, and he passes them on to Mole.

"You know, in all of this, an interesting point is that they hear and understand as they talk to each other," says Fr. John, an Irish priest with whom I have raised the question of the wavering knowledge of Ratty and Mole. Light like fool's motley from the cheap stained glass of a local bar touches his glass of Fosters as he sets it down, considering... "Didn't the music become clearer as they said things like 'what's that?' Yet, you know," he turns the glass and prism like light flashes, "we humans exchange our opinions on almost anything except spiritual perception—why is that, do you think?"

Perhaps we have not often the simplicity of Mole and Ratty Their attention is not to how impossible it is that there be a speaking in the reeds by the water, a speaking more than the chance brushing of air and wood, and not even on how foolish I sound saying I hear a voice in the murmuring or on what the other is hearing and thinking but ever and only, in dim and small brains, on the voice,

"This time, at last, it is the real, the unmistakable thing," murmurs Ratty. And then his attention gone again, he is asleep... with a smile of much happiness on his face, and something of a listening look still lingering there.

XVIII

EDEN AS PAST, FUTURE,
AND PRESENT

PSYCHOLOGISTS TELL US that a child has memories of
the time before birth and a sense of a loss of that peace-
ful time. The human race also remembers the Garden
of Eden from the time before history began and feels a
lost innocence. This is one of the themes of the Orthodox liturgical prayers at the beginning of Lent,
Adam described as weeping outside of paradise, which
he has lost but remembers.

However, this sense of loss and of longing is not the
only way in which the Garden of Eden of Genesis 1–3
remains in the human and Christian imagination.

In this brief sequence, an imaginary Paper perhaps to
adopt a form for it, I will intend to suggest some of the

other dimensions of Eden. We will not intend to deal with a theological question of to what extent "Eden" is lost, except by implication, but to consider its persistent presence to the human imagination and understanding of experience.

Perhaps we might begin with a poem by the New York Jewish poet Charles Reznikoff which Fr. Schmemann loved.

> As I was wandering with my unhappy thoughts,
> I looked and saw
> that I had come into a sunny place, familiar
>   and yet strange.
> "Where am I?" I asked a stranger. "Paradise."
> "Can this be Paradise?" I asked surprised,
> for there were motor cars and factories.
> "It is," he answered. "This is the sun that
>   shone on Adam once;
> the very wind that blew upon him, too.
> —Charles Reznikoff, New York, 1951

Indeed balancing the sense of loss is the realization that after all this is still the world which God made. For the Christian it is Christ who reveals the world as God intended it, so at Vespers of Christmas we sing in the Orthodox Church,

> O come, let us rejoice in the Lord as we de-
> clare this present mystery: The partition wall
> of disunion has been destroyed, the flaming
> sword is turned back, the cherubim withdraw
> from the Tree of Life, and I partake of the food
> of Paradise . . .

And St Maximus, in *Ambigua 41*, includes the reunion of the earth as paradise (Eden) with the human world among the five unifications accomplished in the risen Christ. The others being the union of male and female, of heaven and earth, of the sensible and the intelligible, of the created and the uncreated.

Yet if at moments such as Reznikoff records in his poem, this world and Eden indeed merge, still for the most part we do not feel ourselves in Paradise, or at least not fully and simply so.

Jewish spiritual writing flowered in Spain where gardens were very important in life, in particular of upper class people, and it is through Spain that formal gardens entered Europe. With this background these writers came to see the world we know as sustained by upper and inner gardens... going back to Eden. The Garden, Arthur Green says in summarizing this thought is, "A hidden level within the divine and human being and not just the lost garden of the Biblical story, nor is it only the paradise to which souls will rise after death. Eden is the upper world mirrored in the gardens we know. Garden within garden, the upper ones sustaining the lower..."

The image, the river of continual creation flowing from the Eden above down into our world...

Dante expressed a similar vision in his description of the Earthly Paradise at the top of Mount Purgatory which is the Garden of Eden. It has been placed there to keep it above all the disorder of the level of daily life in the world. Here the wind blows in accord with the movement of the stars. In the great forest of this garden, there are no paths and yet it is easy to find one's way, and Dante sees a pageant procession and then finds two rivers. Drinking from one removes all the bitterness of memory, from the second restores the awareness of good. I think perhaps this section, at the center of the Divine Comedy, is a very rich and important one and one which itself is a garden, delightful to visit.

In recent years in the time of the charismatic renewal, the American hymn writer Andy Park, likely unacquainted with Jewish spirituality or even with Dante, had a sort of vision of a river flowing down from the Mountain of God and he wrote a hymn, which begins...

> "Down the mountain the river flows
> And it brings refreshing wherever it goes
> Through the valleys and over the fields
> The river is rushing and the river is here..."

The sense of Eden as the inner life of things lies behind the English poet Gerard Manly Hopkins's concept of "inscape," of the inwardness of things. Helen Gardner said, "To Hopkins, an inscape was something more than a delightful sensory impression: it was an insight, by divine grace, into the ultimate spiritual reality, seeing the pattern, air, melody, in things from, as it were, God's side." Hopkins liked especially the medieval philosopher Dun Scotus and may have likely understood Scotus's "thisness" of a thing its 'haecceitas' as corresponding to his "inscape."

Perhaps then, in this very brief survey, we have suggested that not only is the Garden of Eden not simply a memory of a human emergence in the past, or on the other hand the projection to the past of a future as it may be, but in Christian and also in Jewish spirituality, it is a level within, implicit within and sustaining of, our reality.

To end with a parallel to Adam weeping outside Paradise here is the poet Robert Lax waiting for a Paradise which is both waited for, and experienced now in the waiting and in the inwardness of things, and which also is remembered.

> I'm looking ahead. Looking towards some point. some vanishing point, or anyway, not yet visible point in the distance, in the future where something or someone I'd recognize would appear. (where you would appear) . . . My person, my beloved, if you like; my sought-after-being, my remembered one, would be there.

The Garden of Eden is always with us, as remembered, as sought after, and as mysteriously present at each moment.

XIX

LABYRINTH
AND FREEDOM

A FELLOW SCIENCE FICTION WRITER wrote of James
Blish, who did, for one thing, a great deal of work
with *Star Trek*, that he loved arcane systems and
labyrinths of mind... *The Garden of Cyrus* of Thomas
Browne, or the *Biographia Literaria* of Coleridge which
was by his bed at the last." He seemed too frail to tra-
verse those gusty corridors of metaphysics. Here was
one more ramshackle structure of thought tempting
him in. But Time with which he had wrestled... had
run out."

On my desk Herman Melville's *The Confidence Man*, an
enigmatic work. Who is the Confidence Man on the
riverboat ? How many pages of it will I read this time

into it? Also I see several books from the Kyoto School of philosophers including *Nothingness and the Religious Worldview* of Kitaro Nishida, founder of that school. I do not know how much of it I will read or understand. And yes, like Blish, I too love Browne and his *Garden of Cyrus*.

Now the literal labyrinth, or maze, which may, in a way, be parallel to an obscure or difficult piece of writing, is something humans have made from beginnings lost in the mists of prehistory. Perhaps also the form of the maze rises from, or at least reminds of, the convoluted turnings of the biological structure of the human brain, and in particular also, with its choices of path to the left or to the right, of the brains two-part, bicameral, nature. We make and seek out mazes because we feel them our natural sort of place rather as if entering a mysterious looking building we recognized it as our own home.

A maze may have many turns and many ends and is a kind of puzzle, but a labyrinth is unicursal, on the other hand, and has one path which followed through however many turns leads to one end. That end may be a place of challenge such as in that famous labyrinth of ancient Crete which Theseus dared and overcame the Minotaur, or also it may be a place of spiritual initiation as many ancient labyrinths represent. It seems that we owe the survival of the ancient labyrinths to monks who worked with the old circular Minoan model, preserving and altering it until it took the form of eleven tracks winding towards a center.

Certain it is also that monastics, beginning with those first who went out into the Egyptian deserts, also sought and entered that silence in which inner paths open which go through more dimensions than are traversed either by outer labyrinth or any maze of traced lines. Indeed the life of mind and heart may seem all puzzling maze with paths that lead here to a dead end, or there to an endless loop, or yet again back out to the beginning. Some inner paths may lead to goals we recognize as our own and yet which attained are but secondary and do not satisfy. Some inner corridors are light and some are dark. The inner world indeed may come to seem a desolate, puzzling place, mere maze of neurons with no real exit, a sort of prison or yet again as barren as the desert those first monks entered.

But the work of the monastic, or of anyone seeking in prayer and work through all the days of life to live life fully and truly is to find and follow on along that path which is not maze but labyrinth . . . all its bends leading on to a center. Perhaps to the "I" beyond "me" of Hillel, or the "god within" of Plotinus, but also even beyond that to the One beyond.

I suppose our experience is both of maze and of labyrinth and of labyrinth within maze as it were. I think of the fascination of the paths of difficult books, and also of the choices that need to be made every day often without any absolute clarity as to where they may lead or which if any of available ways is the best. This is the way it is within our days; within Time. But we have, from the example of the saints who have gone before, but also from our own experience, as it may be, an awareness of a path, labyrinthine but finally straight, which is beneath and beyond all of this and in effect do we not seek on earth, in the most down to earth, that which others before us and even we ourselves, have found in heaven?

The Tang Dynasty poet, and court official, Wang Wei, whose life was one of attempting to balance the affairs of the city with the silence of mountain and forest and the hermitages he sought out, said late in life found it labyrinthine to contemplate and spoke of, "My old forests in which I fear to get lost." Thinking of them, he rehearses some characteristic images of his, tropes, which may show a way "the wind blowing in the pines" ... "a mountain moon my lamp" ... "a river" ... His way marked by such images brings us not to some summary of enlightened awareness but to the edge of mystery in another image, "a fisherman's song deep in the river."

In 1997 on pilgrimage and having slept little after overnight journey by pilgrimage bus, I came to Chartres just at dawn. I walked the Labyrinth set on the floor and came to the center and no special realization and then walked out and saw a round cloud red over the towers of the cathedral.

A little after I wrote this:

> The rose circle in the sky over the towers of Chartres in the early morning air... for just some moments in its color and form and mottled pattern the appearance of that archetype, maybe, which the glass makers tried to capture in the great rose window and yet could not quite... any more than the labyrinth maker could, on the cathedral floor, express its ever moving lines and forms.

Dr. John Pordage's "Abysmal Eye"...

Many walk the Chartres maze and still more perhaps patterns of it traced on paper as I have seen on the floor of church halls, or laid out in gardens, with earnest men and women following the lines, looking for some unimaginable center which arrived at, in those terms, is but another point in ordinary space and another moment in daily time.

But there in the air is the true labyrinth, the mottled shimmering rose of cloud, its patterns and paths ever changing, and now fading over the Cathedral into the morning light... there all the rose light of Tennyson's Grail... there surely the true and straight paths of the true labyrinth... now withdrawing and gone in the glimmering sky...